MW00646922

SHOTGUNS
ON SUNDAY

by
JOSEPH E. DOCTOR

WESTERNLORE PRESS . . . LOS ANGELES 41

COPYRIGHT 1958 BY
WESTERNLORE PRESS

PRINTED IN THE UNITED STATES OF AMERICA BY WESTERNLORE PRESS

ILLUSTRATIONS

SHOTGUNS ON SUNDAY

I

SHOTGUN BLASTS, punctuated with the sharp crack of rifle fire, boomed into the ears of the drink-shaky inhabitants of the bawdy tenderloin of Bakersfield, California, on the sunny Sunday morning of April 19, 1903.

Word spread like a chain-reaction across the flat expanse of the ugly new oil city on the banks of the Kern River. A posse, after weeks of chase, had cornered James McKinney in the Chinese joss house on L street. The long awaited battle was joined. Outlaw and posse-men were shooting it out with shotguns at pointblank range.

On bicycles, on foot, on horseback, in horse-drawn conveyances, Bakersfield's citizens rushed to the scene. They arrived at the joss house to find Jim McKinney already dead, his body draped over the railing at the head of the back stairway leading into the opium den beneath the joss house, blood oozing from the place where the left side of his face had been. Burt Tibbet, smoking shotgun near at hand, was crouched over the prostrate body of his brother, Deputy Marshal Will Tibbet, at the foot of the steps leading to the rear entrance of the building. City Marshal Jeff Packard, still expressing concern for the welfare of his deputy, was being solicitously led away from his place of refuge in the outhouse near the rear entrance, dripping blood from wounds in the neck and both arms.

But the excitement was far from over. Al Hulse, pal of McKinney, was thought to be still in the joss house, and Sheriff James Kelly, leader of the posse, did not propose to lose any more men trying to smoke him out with gunfire. As the surviving possemen remained to lay seige to the building, the curious, the morbid and the concerned among the spectators followed the wounded men to the places they were taken—Tibbet to Baer's drug store four blocks away, and Marshal Packard to his home on 18th street several blocks away. Summoned from their Sunday morning duties, most of the town's doctors converged on the two places to confer with professional importance. Word soon spread through the crowds outside. The doctors said that Tibbet was done for but Packard might be saved. The physicians were half right. Tibbet was done for, all right, and died little more than an hour later; but Packard was also finished. He expired early next morning from shock induced by his wounds.

Although few, if any, of the participants and witnesses were aware of it at the time, the gory battle in the Chinese tong headquarters on Bakersfield's L Street brought to a close an epic period in the American West. Bakersfield looked on the incident as perhaps the most revolting of a series of "man for breakfast" episodes which had given the city a reputation for being the roughest and most hellish of its day, worthy successor to Virginia City, Abilene, Dodge, Deadwood, Tombstone, Bodie and other western boomtowns noted at various times for the vigor of their vice and violence.

Death of Jim McKinney in the lethal blasts from the avenging shotgun of Burt Tibbet was to mark the end of the western badman as an authentic figure in American history. A chronicler of the day, writing in a Bakersfield newspaper, *The Californian,* referred to him as the last of the Old West's outlaw tradition, and expressed no regret at the passing.

The legend of western outlawry which had started with Frank and Jesse James had made a spectacular epoch, but it had run its course, leaving behind a tradition and material for an entire field of American folklore which was to flourish in the dime novel, the horse opera, movie, and later on in radio and television, as well as in the nasal ballads of western folk music.

The Daltons had made a glorious last stand on the streets of Coffeyville, Kansas, while trying to crown their unwholesome success with the holdup of two banks at the same time. California's train robber, Chris Evans, made meek by the loss of an eye and an arm while defending himself from behind a straw pile

● 13

against a reluctant posse, was sitting out a long sentence in San Quentin prison. Curly Bill and others of Old Man Clanton's gang were at eternal peace in the Boot Hill cemetery of Tombstone, Arizona, after burnishing the reputations of Wyatt Earp and the deadly dentist, Doc Holliday, with their blood at the OK Corral. Billy the Kid and the Apache Kid were dead and gone. The Sundance Kid and others of the Wild Bunch had fled to South America. Even Bloody Harry Tracy of Oregon had not long survived the new century and departed, leaving the field to Jim McKinney as the last of the western badmen.

Had he lived in a less enlightened time and setting, McKinney might have become a legendary hero of the stature of Jesse James, and like Jesse, had children of hero-worshipping followers named after him. He had, like James, the likeable personality that brought him the good regard of those with whom he associated, inducing them to overlook the streak of cruel selfishness and ungovernable temper which led him to take the lives of six men, two of them shot down in as cold-blooded an ambush as the West had ever experienced.

Biographers of western badmen have passed McKinney by with scarcely a mention, yet surely he fills a prominent role in the lore and gore of the Old West. Unlike the life stories of most of his predecessors, McKinney's needs not the garnish of fiction and hearsay. The truth about him is awful and exciting enough. He was one of those individuals whose lives are geared to the sensational.

14 •

The spectacular manner in which he departed from the scene was sufficient to merit him a place in the annals of western adventure. For the better part of a year, during a chase over two states and deep into Old Mexico, he was hot copy for the press of California and the Territory of Arizona, and his exploits served as feature material for newspapers all the way to the East Coast. When his capture became imminent, the major newspapers of the West Coast sent their best correspondents to cover the anticipated fight. Three posses of courageous, hard-riding peace officers took his trail, all eager for the reward on his head. In two of the posses were men with a grim, personal antipathy toward McKinney who would have been delighted to battle it out with him in single combat with fists, gun, knife or teeth.

His lack of standing in the lusty literature of the West is due to a number of reasons. He had no single press agent of the calibre of Joaquin Miller or Ambrose Bierce, such as had old Chris Evans and his pal, John Sontag, in their raids on the Southern Pacific Railroad in California. The power of press agentry in sustaining an outlaw's reputation is well demonstrated by the fact that one of the West's best known desperados, Joaquin Murietta, did not exist at all except in the imaginative mind of a learned Cherokee who made him up in a fictional pot-boiler that ultimately passed for truth.

Moreover, the West had begun to mature, and outlaws of McKinney's like were no longer fashionable. Bakersfield was involved in the Cinderella excitement of getting rich practically overnight in oil. The city was perhaps more than a little ashamed of a cheap procurer

• 15

and tinhorn gambler who had stirred up its sense of insecurity by shooting down two of the town's best liked peace officers. Reaction against lawlessness and vice was setting in. While Bakersfield could nurture in its bosom the likes of Jim McKinney and his unwholesome friend, Al Hulse, the city was also at the time the growing-up place for a boy named Earl Warren, destined to become chief justice of the nation's highest court.

There is yet another reason why McKinney has failed to achieve his true place in the romance of the West. It is well expressed in the words of Charles Owens, a Bakersfield old-timer, to one who was probing for facts of the McKinney story fifty years after the fight in the joss house.

"Young fella, if you had been down here in Bakersfield asking questions about Jim McKinney even ten years ago, you could have got yourself shot."

Owens refused to enlarge on the statement, but his inference was that, as parts of the final episode in McKinney's colorful career were never made completely clear, there were those who wanted the story forgotten as quickly as possible. It was always suspected there was a third man in the room in the joss house when Packard and Tibbet burst fatally through the door. Jenny Fox, who was in the room when the shooting started, saw him and described him quite thoroughly, although she was later to deny that he ever existed. She did not know his name, but this is not strange, for despite the many intimacies of Jenny's profession, introductions were not necessary.

16 •

Who, then, was the well dressed, fair-haired man with the moustache whom Jenny described? If, as many suspected, he was a prominent Kern County man, his influence was such that he was never brought to trial, or even placed under arrest, and his name never appeared in the newspapers in connection with the last stand of Jim McKinney.

This, then, is the unembellished story of the last of the western badmen, James McKinney, who wrote his name in a large and confident hand on the numerous court documents of his country in his day, and figuratively wrote it in blood in the history of California's South San Joaquin Valley and Arizona's Mohave County.

One aspect of his life differs from those of his predecessors in western outlawry. Nearly all of them died as young men in their early twenties. Although McKinney started as did most of the others, as a juvenile delinquent, he survived to the age of 42 years before being brought to the final, inevitable accounting.

That his personality was a Jekyll-Hyde arrangement may be determined from the testimonials of those who knew him.

"Finest man you ever met, when he was sober," recalled the late Webb Loyd of Porterville who ran the lunch counter of Scotty's Chop House in McKinney's Porterville days.

"He was a snake, a cold killer who never gave his opponent a chance," said an old pioneer Sierra cattleman who always suspected, but never could prove, that McKinney rustled his cattle.

Those who remember him favorably curse liquor for his downfall. A few blame an over-doting mother for Jim's schizoid personality which led him to the depths. Yet liquor cannot be offered as an excuse for the killing by McKinney of a man and a scarcely grown boy whom he dry-gulched while stone sober on a lonely Arizona road.

His record is plain. He killed four men most certainly, beyond the shadow of a doubt. Two others he killed or helped to kill. His guns and terrible temper were responsible for the wounding of many others. He was a hired gun hand, a pimp, a gambler, a boozer who could not hold his liquor, and finally a merciless killer who had no remorse.

Yet in the tolerant society of the Old West, he had so many friends that he was able to avoid accounting for assault and murder and to live at large for most of a year while being pursued by dozens of highly competent peace officers. Perhaps he would have survived to a ripe old age had Al Hulse been able to resist the temptation to boast to his drinking companions of his knowledge of the outlaw's whereabouts the day before the posse ran him to earth.

Jim McKinney was attractive to women, although the kind he sought and with whom he consorted were not the envy of decent men. A woman helped him break jail; a woman kept him informed of the movements of peace officers who pursued him; a woman was to save his sidekick, Hulse, from the gallows by deciding to remain loyal to him, changing her testimony of the final fatal battle to puncture the state's case against Hulse.

18 ●

Two of three pictures of McKinney known to exist show him as a handsome man of medium stature, a good dresser in a conservative manner. He had fair, curly hair, wide-set, large, cold blue eyes and a smooth complexion. He usually wore a rather long but neat moustache.

He was athletic in build, and as a young man was expert at the rough sport of bronc riding. The first joint of the index finger of his right hand was missing, but it did not interfere with his ability to draw fast and shoot straight.

The last picture of McKinney is a horrible pictorial treatise on the wages of sin. Dissipation and the effects of the long final chase across the desert left him thin and emaciated. The photographer who documented him nude on a slab in the dirty back room of the old Payne & Hansberger mortuary mercifully threw a towel over the loins of the body and shot the picture from the right side. At the time, that was McKinney's best profile, for the left side of his face was a blob of bloody flesh, churned up by the pellets from Burt Tibbet's shotgun.

To the very last, McKinney's friends and his three brothers stuck loyally by him. His brother, Ed, was trying to make a deal for him with the crusty Arizona sheriff even as the posse chased him to his final stand. Ed and many of Jim's friends were convinced to the last that McKinney had not committed the Arizona killings because they could not believe he could commit murder in so cold-blooded a manner. They even excused him for slaying his friend, Billy Lynn, in Porterville the

• 19

year before on the grounds that McKinney had mistaken Lynn for the town marshal, coming to arrest him. In the code of the Old West, it was considered little blame on an outlaw to defend himself against a sheriff.

Half a century after McKinney had paid his debt to society, a respectable man described the outlaw as a "fine person," disregarding or forgetting that the desperado made his living as a gambler, a procurer, a "shotgun man."

"I've seen him change a $10 bill into fifty-cent pieces on Sunday morning so he could stand in front of a saloon to pass out coins to men who had drunk and gambled too much the night before. In those days fifty cents would buy a man breakfast and a drink to pick him up, and Jim saw to it that the down-and-out ones were provided for."

Chester Doyle, who has lived in Porterville virtually all his life, knew McKinney well, for the outlaw stayed for a time in the second floor rooming house Doyle's parents operated in Porterville.

"He was as good a pal as a boy could have, I guess. He used to invite me into his room to watch him clean and oil his guns. It was his custom to carry his revolver stuck in his belt, not in a holster, and the other gamblers who were gun toters did the same," Doyle said.

McKinney was a deadly shot with a six-gun. Kit Tatman, a lithe, lively contemporary and friend of McKinney in his Porterville days, saw many demonstrations of Jim's marksmanship.

"More than one time I have walked out toward the ball park with him, out where there weren't many houses. On the way I'd throw up clods of dirt for him to shoot at. He'd bust 'em every time. He could chase a tin can down the street with bullets from his gun, keeping it moving all the time.

"One day some fellers that hung around the saloons tied a can to a dog's tail and the dog went runnin' down the street. Jim pulled his gun and began firin' at the can, and he never missed once.

"Oh, Jim was some feller—when he wasn't drinkin'!"

Art Kilbreth, who was cooking in Scotty's Chop House the wild night when McKinney ran amuck and shot up Porterville, backed the statement of his friend, Kit Tatman, that McKinney usually exhibited a fine personality.

"He was a perfect gentleman to wait on in the chop house," Kilbreth said. "I never had a better or more courteous customer. Nice and quiet. Even when he had a complaint to make, he did it in a nice way."

Kit Tatman also remembered McKinney's weaker moments. He was present in Dave Mosier's Mint Saloon one night when McKinney was playing seven-up for $20 a game. His opponent, a man considerably older than McKinney, won with such consistency that Jim, who was drinking, completely lost his temper, pulled his gun, and began striking at the older man with the barrel of it.

An on-looker who tried to protest the pistol-whipping found himself looking into the business end of the weapon as Jim turned on him. He attempted to beat a hasty retreat and started so suddenly his feet slipped from under him. He scrambled on all fours along the floor toward the door, and McKinney sped him along by firing into the floor behind him.

"That happened after the killing of Red Sears in Bakersfield," Tatman said, "and after that he always carried two guns. He was always careful not to let both of them get empty at the same time."

McKinney was born in Illinois in 1861, when the legend of the Wild West was just beginning. He grew up in the West, following the settlements toward the setting sun as sin and vice followed the trail blazers. He closed the chapter in California's San Joaquin Valley, as far west as the wild part of it could go, for beyond were the sleepy old towns of the coast, just throwing off the lethargy bequeathed to them by their Spanish founders.

McKinney's first stomping ground in California was Visalia, established in 1852 in the fertile delta of the Kaweah River which drains from the Sierra Nevada mountains, flowing westward into the San Joaquin Valley. Visalia was settled early in the valley's history, and like all western towns which depended on cattle and wheat for their prosperity, it was a rough place. Its teamsters, harvest hands, gamblers and pimps carried six-guns until the turn of the century. Its decent citizens had a time or two been driven to lynching to keep the wild ones in check. It had far more saloons than churches. It had a thriving red light district and gambling dens at the rear of every bar where woodsmen, cattlemen and prospectors from the nearby mountains, and teamsters and harvest hands from the flatlands, might blow their accumulated wages to the eager enticement of as colorful, convincing a collection of gamblers and prostitutes as any western town could boast. Thirty miles to the south, on Tule River, was Porterville, where McKinney set himself up when his welcome wore out in the county seat, Visalia. Porterville was a somewhat smaller copy of Visalia and was, if anything, even more devoted to the pleasures of night life. It was often referred to as Pokerville, because to many that seemed to be its principal business. As for its other pleasures, M. J. O'Clancy, the editor of the old *Porterville Enterprise*, the leading journal of the community in its day, was once moved to complain that the red light district had become so crowded that one madam had set up shop next to the *Enterprise* office, to the considerable embarrassment of Mrs. O'Clancy when she came to visit her husband's place of business. The scarlet ladies often sat in their windows to catch the cool breezes during the daytime when they were not otherwise occupied.

McKinney gave impetus to the eventual reformation of Porterville when he shot up the terrified and helpless town single-handed on a hot night in the summer of 1902.

McKinney's last refuge was in Bakersfield, on Kern River, 50 miles south of Porterville, one of the last resorts of badmen, pimps and gamblers. To it fled the depraved characters of the mordant Barbary Coast of San Francisco during the periodic, indignant housecleanings of that city. Oofty Goofty, the well known Pacific Street barfly, was known to the Bakersfield tenderloin. He was famous in San Francisco for his length

• 23

of billiard cue and his tough hide. For the price of a drink, he would let the bar customers whack his podex as hard as they wished with the billiard cue, and he endured many a lusty blow. Bakersfield old-timers also remember another Barbary Coast character, Mule Face Kelly, whose visage so resembled that of the West's principal beast of burden that he was able to win drinks just by permitting the boys at the brass rail to look at him and laugh.

Not only from the Barbary Coast, but also from rugged Arizona, still a territory, came the boomtown riff-raff, seeking refuge and a living in the oil city as the mines in Arizona played out.

Bakersfield had some characters of its own minting. Kelly the Rake, an eccentric gambler, and Big Bertha, a hefty chunk of femininity who ran the town's most popular variety hall, were typical.

Bakersfield, as the last survivor of the tough towns of the Old West was, in the opinion of those who had seen its predecessors, by all odds the toughest. In the Kern River country of the Sierra Nevada to the east, in Inyo County east of the Sierra divide, and in the deserts to the southeast, gold was discovered after the Mother Lode to the north had begun to wane. Kern County's mines acquired a good many drifters who were chased from the north by vigilantes. Havilah, Whiskey Flat, Isabella, Keysville and Glennville in Kern County, and Tailholt, just over the border in Tulare County, became outposts of the Gold Rush. Later in Death Valley and the Mojave Desert the miners turned to borax, copper and silver, but their ways did not soften.

24 •

The cowboys, rootin', tootin', and shootin' as they were in Arizona and Texas, came also to the Kern country, the evil with the just plain boisterous. Cattle rustling was so prevalent in the foothills east of Bakersfield late in the last century that many legitimate cattlemen were forced out of business and others were forced to employ special guards. The West's traditional "one old steer and a good running iron" were the foundations of many a herd. It was in good tradition, for one of the South San Joaquin Valley's earliest white residents was the old Mountain man, Pegleg Smith, who came to Buena Vista Lake early in the 19th century to harass the Spanish on the coast with his horse-stealing proclivities.

But it was neither gold nor cattle that was to set off Bakersfield as a boomtown. It was oil. A smouldering fuse of drilling had existed in the county for forty years before the turn of the century, financed by bold, chance-taking money from the gold country. The demand for coal oil for lamps was insufficient to instigate a boom, and it was not until the dawn of the 1900's, when a sensational oil strike on the Kern River corresponded with the move of the railroads to convert from coal to petroleum to fire their boilers, that Bakersfield became a mecca for the get-rich-quick set. Chugging along the dusty roads, scaring horses and providing pleasure for rich playboys, was the internal combustion powered gas buggy that used a waste product of petroleum for fuel.

The Kern River discovery corresponded with the sudden upswing in the demand for oil. In the brief per-

• 25

iod of a few weeks new millionaires were made and others were as quickly broken. Overnight Bakersfield filled up with big-money speculators. Everyone who could finance a lease and a rig put down a well. Drillers from Pennsylvania, Illinois and the Southern California fields, a hard-handed bunch who fought with Stillson wrenches and soaked up their pay in whiskey every Saturday night, flocked to the Kern fields. They were joined by hatchet-wielding rig builders, tool dressers, roughnecks, pipeline layers, teamsters and a myriad of common laborers needed to convert the Kern County potential into the West's richest oil field.

In the grab for oil lands, lease wars broke out. So prevalent was lease jumping that major companies hired gun hands, "shotgun men," to guard their properties. This kind of work came naturally to Jim McKinney, who had been a ditch guard in the water wars earlier in Tulare County.

The activity in the new oilfield was matched in scope by Bakersfield's night life, especially in the tenderloin. One of the early civic boasts of Bakersfield was a streetcar system, and it did a thriving business. On Saturday nights when the men came in from the fields for fun and relaxation, the streetcars were so crowded that as late as midnight and even into the small hours of Sunday, men hung outside and even on top. In the tenderloin, a dozen different dance halls furnished pretty girls and entertainment. In the gambling dens, men waited for places at the tables and the chance to give away their money. There were cribs in every block; a man had his choice of many ages, degrees of pulchritude,

26 •

and a variety of nationalities, except Chinese, for the price of one dollar. Only Chinese men were allowed in the Chinese cribs.

An oil developer of that period has reported that because of the variety of pleasures Bakersfield offered, it was often difficult to carry on the work in the fields. Oil companies actually failed because they could not hold their workers against the lures of the palaces of sin. A company with a hundred workers in production during the week would be lucky to get ten back on Monday morning after a riotous weekend in Bakersfield.

Murder and strong-armed robbery were frequent. The habitués of the tenderloin were also highly skilled in the less violent methods of separating a man from his money. The pretty girls in the dance halls flim-flammed their boy friends of the evening with artful resources. The clincher, if all else failed, was a well loaded "mickey" to pass a man out so that he might be rolled for his money.

Girls in the cribs had talents other than those related to sex. "That one dollar doesn't seem like much of a price today, and it wasn't then," a man well acquainted with the tenderloin recalled many years later. "The dollar was often just sort of a token payment. Once a man was inside, he frequently paid all he had, as there was someone in attendance to go through the pockets of his pants while he wasn't using them. Some of the boys took the precaution of hanging them at the head of the bed, but the madam usually had a hole and a false panel in the wall near the head of the bed through which to reach and go through the pants pockets.

"Then there was the favored customer treatment. A man would be welcomed on several occasions, entertained to his satisfaction for the going price, and made to feel as if he were a special favorite because of his charm. Then one night he'd show up with a pocket full of money, maybe with several friends, and they'd fleece him and his companions out of all they had.

"A man caught in a situation like that doesn't complain to the law, so the girls were safe. No one had much sympathy for the men who were rolled, anyway. If you hung around the tough part of town, you were supposed to be able to take care of yourself."

The good wages paid in the oil fields brought wealth to many persons engaged in the tenderloin's various businesses. Big Bertha's dance hall profits were such that she wore only gowns made from the finest silks imported from China. Gamblers were able to finance oil speculation and many became wealthy, ultimately engaging in more respectable businesses.

As the virtuous women of the town never ventured into the tenderloin, the only time they had the opportunity to see the gaudy exterior of the wages of sin was on circus day, when the girls put on their finery and came down to Chester, the broad main street, to exhibit their wares and watch the parade. There were so many that they occupied three entire blocks of curb space.

"They were far more interesting to us than the elephants and the clowns," commented a respectable woman who can remember watching them from the opposite side of the street. "It was the only time we got a look at them."

The gamblers were the overlords of the tenderloin. Oil promotion was then even more highly speculative than it is today. Fifty years ago the banks financed the most solvent operators, and the railroads helped others, but by far the biggest source of loans to the wildcatters was the big gambler. He had ready money and the courage to risk it. He also had, as long as the men came in from the oil fields to try their hands at dice and cards, a steady supply. He took security if he could get it, none if he had faith in the promoter.

The gamblers were also a prime source of charity. Theirs was the heaviest contributions for the down-and-outer or for the burial of the latest victim of gunplay.

Violent death was common in the tenderloin. Men, and less frequently women, died of gunshot, clubbings, stabbings, acute and chronic alcoholism, and dope. The coroner's inquest records covering the first years of the century are an excellent study of the case histories of sudden and sordid demise in infinite variety, down to the last gruesome details. The coroner's job was one of the busiest in Bakersfield.

Chinese were numerous in the Bakersfield tenderloin, their centers of society being the tong headquarters which were called joss houses by the Occidentals. There were at least three of these houses in Bakersfield in 1900, including the one on L Street where McKinney made his last stand. Chinese ran lotteries, laundries, and restaurants, or peddled vegetables about the community. Many a supposedly legitimate business was a

● 29

front for an opium den in the basement. In them the hard-working, low-paid Orientals who toiled in the fields, on the railroad, in the mines, and as domestics found relaxation in the ecstasy of poppy dreams. They were hardened against the effects of addiction by generations of selective survival. When white men came to smoke and dream, as many did, they risked physical and mental disaster. Just as the Indian cannot withstand the effects of the white man's firewater, so the white man has not the constitution for the delights of the Oriental poppy. Numerous white inhabitants of the Bakersfield tenderloin became addicted to narcotics, as they were easy to obtain in the Chinese sector. Whites who used narcotics frequently became involved in Chinese society, tolerated by the patient Chinese who supplied them with drugs and awaited the eventual and inevitable disintegration.

The scions of prominent Bakersfield families were not immune. Seeking the adventures of the tenderloin, some of them, too, ended up in addiction. Their families might deplore the civic sore that had infected their sons, but they could do little about it for fear of scandal.

The accounting of the wages for all this sin is well preserved in the records of the Kern County coroner. One dismal Monday morning he had no fewer than eleven bodies over which to preside, a number that would have done credit to a city many times the size of Bakersfield. All were unattended deaths. It was the coroner's job to find out how death arrived, and from his records the district attorney could determine if the cause of death warranted a prosecution.

SHOTGUNS ON SUNDAY

Billy Carder, born in the town of Columbia when it was the queen of California's placer gold mining communities, was brought up in the tough Mother Lode country. As a young man he moved to Bodie and spent two years as a faro dealer in a leading gambling hall. Small in stature and an expert with horses, Billy was much in demand as a jockey when horse racing was the biggest sport in the California and Nevada silver camps, and he visited nearly all of them. He was well qualified as an expert on the relative liberality of the communities in which he worked and lived.

At the age of 98, when he was still keen of mind and filled with the recollections of his youth, Billy was asked which town of all those he knew he considered the most violent and immoral.

"Bakersfield," he answered without hesitation. "Why god-dammit man, I took two wagons and eight horses and went down there to team during the Kern River boom in 1900. You never saw anything like it. There were as many people on the street at 2 o'clock in the morning as there were at noon. Bodie always boasted of its 'man for breakfast,' but it couldn't hold a candle to Bakersfield when it came to shootings.

"I was camped out on the river north of town. One night I was late getting back from a trip and came through Bakersfield with my team about ten o'clock. Down in the main part of the tenderloin I saw a couple doing what they hadn't ought to right out in the street, without even bothering to move away from the street light. And stranger still, people passing by were paying

• 31

very little attention to them. I never saw anything like that up in the Mother Lode country, and I never saw anything like it in Bodie, either."

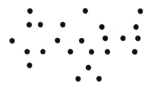

JIM MCKINNEY, ABOUT 1890

II

THE GENESIS of the legend and tradition that sprang up around the western badman is absorbing alike for the student of law, psychology, sociology and history. Generations of small fry have been captivated by the adventurous saga through dime novels, movies, radio and television. The essential plot is primitive and trite, given credence through repetition, appealing to the unsophisticated. There is the excitement of the flight and the chase, the fist fight, the melodramatic threat to the heroine, her ultimate rescue and the final battle up through the rocks, the villain finally lying dead in the dust or being led away by the sheriff while the hero exchanges tender glances with his girl. Persons who never saw a real cowboy or even a civilized Indian have felt the attraction of this variation of folk legendry of the good guys versus the bad guys.

Students of the Wild West attempt to limit its duration from the close of the Civil War to the opening of the Twentieth Century, the Gasoline Age, by which time most of the west had been largely subjected to exploitation and civilization. It must be admitted, however, that the roots go more deeply into American history—back even to the highwayman of old England. Robin Hood might lay aside his bow and arrow and doff his cap of forest green, belt on a pair of six-guns and put on a ten-gallon Stetson and fit the pattern neatly. Early America had its badmen, but it was not until after the Civil War that the heroic type came into being. Jesse James was the prototype, and today many American males whose roots are in the Ozark states are named after him, the phony folk hero who, in legend, stole from the rich to give to the poor. In certain communities the notoriety of the Dalton gang will be better known, and perhaps even better respected, by future generations, than a real hero from the Midwest, Dwight Eisenhower. It is difficult to reach the believers with the truth: that Jesse was not a Robin Hood out to right the wrongs of the poor and downtrodden, but shot down innocent men in cold blood, leaving widows and children to mourn; that the targets for his raids were rich railroads and banks because they had the most of what Jesse desired, money. And the victims of his guns were not the railroad tycoons or the wealthy bankers, but rather the expressmen in the baggage cars and the wage-earning clerks who worked in the banks.

34 •

Blame for the evil, unscrupulous gunmen who entered the West after the Civil War is laid to the fact that this bloody conflict steeped young men scarcely in their teens in violence. James, as was many a youth who later became notorious for his skill with guns and willingness to take human life, was a bushwhacker, a guerrilla, in the Civil War. He rode with Quantrill, the bold Missourian whose brutal raids on the border state of Kansas live in infamy. To those who served in the regular armies of the North and South, the Civil War was a cruel and merciless conflict of brother against brother, well suited to hardening men to accept almost any situation as justification for violation of the Commandment against the taking of life. To those who served as irregulars in the border conflict, it was even worse; not only cruel, but murderous.

Students of western history also blame the cattlemen's bad year of 1874, when herds of cattle perished in blizzards or in the drought which followed, for giving impetus to the lawlessness which helped to set the pattern of western tradition. Impoverished cowpokes, out of work, turned to their six-guns as tools for the making of ready cash. Trains and stage coaches ran across the west, bearing payrolls and easterners who had money and gold watches in their pockets and rings on their fingers. All a man needed to get into business was guts, a gun, and a fast horse.

The first white invaders of the West, the mountain men who went after beaver for the hats of Europe, were a tough lot who cared little for law or life. Mortality among them was high. The mere act of survival under conditions they faced was an achievement. Trapping the beaver, pelting them, and transporting the pelts over hundreds of miles of wilderness trails in the midst of Indians who could never be trusted, made the big money of the fur trade well earned. Most of the trappers were illiterate adventurers who knew little and cared less for the comforts of civilization. Their great virtue was raw courage, which men respect and admire even when the rest of the individual's nature is savage in the extreme. The ultimate compliment that could be paid a man of their company was that he died game. They were practical stoics.

Those who followed the Gold Rush trails to the West after the mountain men had marked them were also men of courage. It took fortitude to quit the quiet security of the eastern farm, store, or office and strike out into the savage West, where Indians warred on the whites and renegades of all colors preyed on the law-abiding. The West drew young men who wanted freedom from law and restraint as well as those who wanted new opportunity. After the Civil War, the restlessness of youth imbalanced by conflict found an outlet across the Mississippi. The migration to the west was implemented by the opportunists, the liquor vendor, the gambler, the prostitute, and the gunman. The denominator common to all was courage.

Second only to courage as an essential to survival in the raw new land was a knowledge of firearms and an ability to use them with skill. The life of the mountain man oft depended on how well he could use the one shot in his long rifle and how fast he could reload. After

36 •

the Civil War came the repeating rifle, which broke the strength of the Indians, and the famous Colt line of hand guns, which became the companion of the cowboy, the outlaw and the gambler.

The weapon of the West which has never been allotted its true place in either history or fiction, because of its lack of romantic appeal, is the unglamorous shotgun. It is highly probable that the double-barreled, short variety often referred to as "sawed off," killed more men in the Old West than did the six-shooter. It was a favorite weapon with outlaws who worked at close range with their victims. It was favored also by peace officers faced with the unpopular task of fighting it out with holed-up outlaws. The regard the man who rode with the driver on the stagecoach to protect the passengers and cargo had for the shotgun is expressed in the term for his job, "riding shotgun." In that classic battle at the OK Corral in Tombstone, it was Doc Holliday's trusty shotgun that fired the first decisive shots. At close range, the .10 or .12 gauge shotgun was the deadliest weapon the Old West knew. In the excitement of the pitched battle at close quarters, men seldom were sufficiently cool to give full effectiveness to the rifle or revolver, but even a jittery individual could score with the scattergun. The best rifleman could not hit the broad side of a barn with a rifle from the pitching top of a stagecoach, but with his weapon the "shotgun rider" could keep the pursuers at bay while the driver whipped the team down the road for safety.

Moreover, the shotgun discouraged retaliation. Many a man plugged through and through with bullets from

• 37

rifle or revolver rose to fight again even as his life ran out, but the man hit in the guts, chest, neck or head with a slug of shotgun pellets was very likely to quit fighting at the instant and surrender up his ghost with scarcely a sigh or a gurgle.

Without firing a shot, the man who had the drop on his enemy with the shotgun had a distinct advantage, for the fellow on the other end, no matter how brave, gazed with hollow-stomached horror into two large, dark tunnels, out of which Death might come at any instant. To carry anything but a hand gun into a bank in the old days was to advertise to one and all that a man expected to emerge richer than he entered, so the six-gun was the favored weapon with bank bandits. Occasionally, however, desperadoes carried shotguns inside their coats on bank jobs, so high a value did they place on the persuasiveness of the weapon.

When Jim McKinney, who was to do his most effective killing with a shotgun, died at the hands of a man armed with a shotgun, a newspaper writer of the day referred to him as "the last of an evil breed." He and his kind had passed beyond the desire of society to protect them. The West, in its immaturity, had tolerated his kind with a sort of childish admiration; but as maturity came, the desperado had to go, just as when maturity comes to the world generally, war will be banished. An occasional revival of conditions which permitted the desperado to exist in the West comes in modern cities. Even intelligent, enlightened individuals have boasted of their acquaintance, even friendship, with gangsters.

38 •

While the West was in its formative stage, McKinney and his predecessors were able to travel about with immunity and to rest securely in the homes of those who befriended them. Acquaintances not only did not inform on their movements, but actually set up a loosely organized but effective intelligence to give the badmen information on efforts of the law to apprehend them. One of the first rules of the Old West was to mind one's own business. Catching outlaws was the sheriff's job, and no affair of those who lived on isolated ranches, subject to the swift and deadly vengeance from the outlaw or his friends in the event they informed. A man could not just step to the telephone and call a policeman when he got in trouble, so he was wise to stay out of it. If an outlaw with a price on his head stopped by, it was best to invite him in for a meal, rustle up some oats for his weary horse, and say nothing after he had gone.

Being a gunman had its attractions for the young and adventurous. It offered freedom, ready cash, and liberty to consort with women of dubious moral virtue, always appealing to men. The outlaw was known to all and commanded an attitude of awe, if not of respect, among his fellows.

It was no deterrent to its practitioners that the end was almost always an ignominious death at an early age and a vast waste of human resource that might have been channelled into respectable achievements. The outlaw always had visions of making his pile and going south of the border to lead a quiet life with the woman of his choice. It seldom happened. Jesse James dead with a bullet in his back, Billy the Kid perforated with slugs from the sheriff's six-gun, Chris Evans enduring a maimed, half-blind existence in prison, and Jim Mc-Kinney slumped on the stairs of an opium den were far from being the romantic figures they were when dashing hell-bent down a dusty road on spirited horses, blazing gun in one hand and a bag of loot in the other, perhaps to keep a tryst with some fair damsel in a hideout.

III

J AMES MCKINNEY was born as the first battles of the Civil War were being fought. His father, Andrew McKinney, was a respectable, hard-working individual whose peregrinations kept him from accumulating money and may have been due largely to the necessity of keeping his family ahead of his eldest son's reputation.

Andrew named this first son after his own father, James McKinney, a migrant to Illinois from Ireland. Andrew's wife, Jim's mother, had relatives both in Missouri and Canada. Those who knew her in her old age describe her differently. To some she was a sweet, lovable person whose only shortcoming was her overprotectiveness for her errant son; to others she was un-

• 41

gentle and quick tempered, a fiery person who abetted her juvenile delinquent by openly praising his rebellious and deadly nature.

"Jim's a good boy, but he'll kill when in drink," she is quoted as saying. The woman to whom she addressed the remark was never quite sure whether it was said as an excuse for her son's actions or in praise of them.

She bore Andrew three other sons, Matt, a meek and delicate little person, Edwin, who became a prosperous saloon man and a loyal protector of his older brother, and Jake, who engaged less legitimately in the liquor business as a bootlegger, but who also stood by Jim when the chips were down.

In the 1870s, the family moved from Illinois to Missouri, where Jim grew to manhood. As Jesse and Frank James were the heroes of Missouri farm folk and lead miners of that decade, it is possible that it was during this time that McKinney adopted the pattern for his future life. Certainly the idolatry with which a good many Missourians regarded the James brothers could have been a powerful influence on a high-spirited youngster such as Jim McKinney.

Oldtimers who knew his family have intimated that McKinney had precedence for outlawry in his own ancestors.

"Jim, you'll end up getting shot, because you are just like your uncle, and he died that way," a man is said to have advised the young man shortly after his arrival in California. The man presumably was acquainted with some of Jim's eastern relatives.

42 •

During the great struggle for newspaper sidelights at the time of McKinney's last sensational gun battle, a reporter for the *Bakersfield Californian* dredged up from some unknown source a story that McKinney was, on his mother's side, a descendant of one Sy Davidson, a notorious, rollicking Missouri frontier hellion who was the terror of Cass County. This character, not out of malice or in hope of monetary gain, but out of sheer exuberance, liked to shoot up towns and terrorize the citizens. His practical jokes contained more violence than humor, and folks became intolerant of him. A typical episode related to his disruption of the solemn ceremony for the laying of a cornerstone for a public building in a Missouri town. The Masonic fraternity was conducting the rites with fitting dignity when Sy came whooping up, gun in hand, and made the Masons open up the copper box and exhibit its contents before plac- ing it in the cornerstone. When Sy was drowned while making a brave but foolish attempt to cross a flooded stream, Cass County heaved a sigh of relief and turned out gratefully *en masse* to attend his funeral.

As it is recorded that Andrew, the father, worked as a miner in Missouri, it is not surprising to find the family next in Leadville, Colorado, which, if Andrew was seeking an atmosphere of virtue in which to raise his four sons, was the wrong place to go. The lusty carbonate camp was a hell-roarer in the true western fashion. Colorado's contribution to the gun-totin' cameraderie of the West was already impressive. Leadville not only played host to thieves and robbers of many descriptions, but also acquired a fraternity of gamblers and a

• 43

frilly sorority of immoral floozies who preyed on the
miners. An old directory of Leadville lists the McKinneys as residents of that city from 1878 to 1880. Andrew's occupation was that of teamster, while the boys
old enough to work, Jim and Jake, are listed as laborers.
They lived at 506 Eighth Street, a middle-class neighborhood at the time.

In all probability it was in Leadville that McKinney
was involved in his first gun fight, although this will
probably never be known for certain. It is known that
he left Leadville for California, where he had relatives,
before the rest of his family migrated. It was the opinion
of those who knew him when he first came to California
that he was then a fugitive, whether from law or vengeance they never found out. Mrs. McKinney was
heard to speak in later years of a gunfight in Leadville
involving Jim, and in which his opponent took refuge
in a blacksmith shop.

"Jim would have killed the son-of-a-bitch, too, if he
had stepped out and fought like a man," was the way
she evaluated the fight to a neighbor in California.

Perhaps Jim took part in the great exodus from Leadville in 1879, when the better element became incensed
over repeated acts of violence and resorted to vigilante
tactics to purge the town of its undesirables. In this
mop-up, the vigilantes set the traditional horrible example by stringing up publicly a couple of the worst
evil-doers. The hasty departure of others was so thorough that the carbonate camp was seldom troubled
thereafter. With his known affiinity for liquor, guns and
trouble, McKinney may have been among those invited

to go. A more charitable excuse for his migration might be to lay it to the second great exodus Leadville was to experience in the following year, when strikes shut down the mines for many months and a good many individuals were forced to go elsewhere to find work. A man with no better occupation than that of laborer, which was McKinney's classification in the old directory, would have had a difficult time.

Whatever the reason for his continuing westward, Jim showed up in the little town of Farmersville, Tulare County, near Visalia, in California's fertile San Joaquin Valley early in 1880. Several months later his parents and younger brothers arrived, traveling in a light wagon drawn by "as pretty a team of mules as was ever seen in this part of the valley," according to a man who eyewitnessed the arrival.

They stayed for a time with John Bell, a relative, who intimated to his neighbor, W. G. Pennebaker, that the family was from a tough town, Leadville, and he hoped their deportment would be in keeping with the quiet spirit of the little community to which they had migrated. The menfolks of McKinney's family worked on Pennebaker's Giant Oak ranch, which occupied several hundred acres of creek bottom soil and was devoted to the growing of alfalfa, grain, and livestock.

Sherman Pennebaker, son of W. G., was among the first California acquaintances of the man who was to become the West's last badman.

"I drove plow team with Jim all one winter," said Sherm, who was named after his father's Civil War commanding officer. "He was a pleasant young feller,

• 45

somewhat older than me, quiet and soft-spoken. He was a good worker and the only way you'd know he had a wild streak in him was that he allus wore a six-shooter, even when he worked. It had a white bone or ivory handle. He could use it, too. He was allus practicin'.

"One day I asked him why he carried a gun. 'Some fellers is lookin' for me,' he told me, 'and when they find me I want to be ready.' "

Pennebaker interpreted this statement as meaning McKinney had been in serious trouble in Leadville and was either afraid of being arrested or of being attacked by persons who sought redress for some injury McKinney had done them.

When the McKinney family reached the San Joaquin empire, it was in the middle period of its early development. Destined to become the nation's richest irrigated farming domain, this vast basket, rimmed on the west by the Coast Range, on the south by the Tehachapi Mountains and on the east by the towering Sierra Nevada, had drawn to its bosom those who had found California's true gold in the fertile fields and salubrious climate. Its gentle Indians had yielded without lifting a scalp before the white man's diseases—more effective than bullets.

The valley was not to give up its riches completely without a struggle. It is poorly watered by nature. Its annual rains, milked grudgingly from winter storms by the mountains to the east, fall only in the winter and spring, and then in quantity sufficient only to qualify the land as semi-arid. Some of the valley's western and

46 •

southern extremities are as arid as the bitter Mohave Desert just beyond the Tehachapis. From the snow-capped Sierra flow occasional streams which, on reaching the table-flat expanse of the valley, finger out into numerous, oft-changing channels which eventually terminate in the swampy sink called Tulare Lake. It was once the broadest expanse of fresh water wholly within the United States, and around its borders grew the immense thickets of reeds called tules, which led the early California Spanish to refer to the entire valley as "Los Tulares." The lake is now only a memory, with rich stands of cotton, grain and alfalfa covering the black soil of the old lake bottom.

Settlers drifting down from the Mother Lode mines to the north in the 1850s and '6os settled along the water courses, the Kings, Kaweah, Tule and Kern rivers. First they dry-farmed grain, but found that by diverting water from the streams they could grow irrigated crops fabulous in variety and yield. The fruitful fig tree, planted at nearly every pioneer doorstep, gave promise of the subtropical horticulture that was to come.

With the coming of the railroads in the early 1870s, the farmers were provided with an eastern outlet for their crops. Dry-farmed grain spread out away from the stream courses over the valley floor. Huge combined harvesters, using as many as 36 head of horses or mules for power, were built. The day of the teamster was in full glory. When he was not plowing, sowing, or harvesting grain in the valley, he could work at hauling lumber from the mills in the mountains nearby.

• 47

Water from the rivers became precious. There was
not enough to go around, and as homesteads grew in
number, men fought over the right to divert the flow of
the streams to their acres. Violence at the headgates of
the ditches became common. Ranchers had need for
hired gun hands to protect the life-blood of their sea-
son's work. Men with the reputation and willingness
for violence were in demand. Decades of legal finagling
were to go on, enriching the attorneys before the final
decisions were made, and they have not all been determined yet.

The valley's first crop was cattle which grew in pro-
lific herds on the rich grasses of the foothills, valley, and
marshes of the lake. The California *vaquero*, a tough
and fiercely independent hombre of Spanish-Indian
descent, and the American cowboy rode herd on the
wild, longhorn Spanish cattle. The herds were driven
to market to the coastal ports, where a prime steer sold
for $2.50, valuable chiefly for the hide and tallow which
could be shipped around the Horn to the east coast.

When the railroads came, wheat became king, and
the teamster joined the *vaquero* and the cowpoke in
spending wages in the saloons and gambling dens of
the dusty frontier towns. Not until the Twentieth Century arrived did the scientific farmer take over, drilling
wells to tap the underground water for new riches, and
setting out vineyards, orchards of deciduous fruits, and
groves of oranges and olives. By that time, there was no
longer a place for McKinney and his kind.

During the Wild West era between the 1860s and
the new century, the valley boasted as degenerate a

48 •

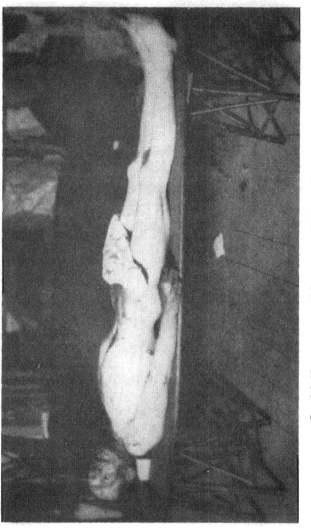

JIM MCKINNEY ON A MORTUARY SLAB IN BAKERSFIELD

collection of desperados, road agents, outlaws and bad-men as any area of the west. During the Civil War and in the years immediately following, trading on a glow of southern sympathy which prevailed in the San Joa-quin, they operated almost with immunity. Mason and Henry caused their share of trouble along the wagon roads. Tiburcio Vasquez conducted raids on the valley from his Coast Range hide-out.

In the 1870s Visalia became so fed up with one of its wayward citizens, Jim McCrory, that it lynched him from the railing of the bridge that spanned the town creek. McCrory had been so ungrateful as to shoot a bartender who had loaned him $10 on which to get drunk. The outlaw was supposed to have had a dozen notches in his gun for men he had killed, not counting Indians, Chinese, and Mexicans, of course.

The valley is said to have had a visit from the notori-ous James brothers, Frank and Jesse, in the late seven-ties. Frank was recovering from a bullet wound re-ceived in one of their midwestern raids when he and his brother came to California to visit their uncle who lived at Paso Robles and to look for the grave of their errant preacher father, who had fallen a victim of dis-ease while on a futile trek to the California gold fields in the early 1850s.

There is a legend which relates that during the per-iod of this California visit two strangers, obviously brothers, came to spend the summer at the little inn kept by Mrs. Cramer at her home in the Tule River foothill country east of Porterville. One of the affable pair appeared to get around with difficulty, using a

• 49

cane, and spent most of his daylight hours under the fig tree that shaded the Cramer yard. If he was not there, his brother was,.and a rifle was always close at hand. Occasionally a passer-by, perhaps a former resident of Missouri or Arkansas on his way to the mountains, gave a startled look of recognition on passing the pair, but had the sense to keep his mouth shut. After they had gone, it was whispered that the two were the James boys, and they had chosen this remote valley in which to rest so that Frank might recover from his wound.

The Daltons, as most Oklahomans sooner or later do, found their way to the San Joaquin also. When the Southern Pacific rail lines in the valley broke out with a rash of bold holdups, the technique of Grat Dalton and his brothers was recognized. Brother Bill Dalton was soon in jail in Visalia. Indignant at such lack of hospitality, he kicked his way through a flimsy wall one night and fled back to Kansas to keep his date with death on the dusty streets of Coffeyville.

Cussedness and deviltry in the San Joaquin were to be best personified by three other knights of the iron road. A pair of evil brothers from Wisconsin, named Sontag, drifted into the valley in the 1890s and joined up with a genial Irishman, Chris Evans, who was having trouble supporting his family and living in the affluence which he desired. Trading on the general unpopularity of the railroad, these characters carried on a lucrative war of attrition against the valuables carried by the trains. With the aid of the press agent wizardry of such noted journalists as Joaquin Miller and Ambrose

Bierce, who were working for San Francisco news-papers, they became the most celebrated outlaws of their day.

George Sontag was soon placed in San Quentin, but Chris and John remained at large until they were finally ambushed by a posse at the foot of a foothill pass near a place called Stone Corral. John Sontag was fatally wounded and Chris, badly shot up with one eyeball dangling on his cheek and one arm mutilated, escaped by walking seven miles at night through the rough hills to the home of a relative. After this almost superhuman effort, he lacked the stamina to resist further and gave himself up to submit to amputation of his arm.

Chris was tried, and while awaiting sentence in the Fresno County jail, he managed to make his escape. An accomplice, a waiter in the restaurant which brought him his meals in jail, served up a six-gun on a tray for supper one evening, and Chris and the waiter, Ed Mor-rel, made a getaway. After a winter in the mountains, tough old Chris Evans decided to call it quits and set-tled for a less strenuous life behind prison walls.

In one respect, McKinney differed from the usual run of outlaws. He was not primarily a bandit. Only when he was hemmed in by his pursuers toward the end of his career and it became necessary to obtain money to finance his flight from a determined sheriff, did he become a hold-up man. Then he killed ruth-lessly and looted the fallen bodies without bothering to give his victims the traditional choice of their money or their lives.

The complete story of McKinney's construction of his evil reputation in California is lacking, because most of the early charges against him were misdemeanors, tried in courts whose records have vanished. Simple fighting and flourishing of weapons were not superior court cases unless the consequences were of a serious nature, and it was not until 1889 that the superior court of Tulare County had filings against McKinney, although he had made the judicial bigtime in Merced County before then. However, his reputation was such that by the time he was hailed into the Tulare County Superior Court, the judge flung the book at him.

His early misdeeds must be compiled from incomplete newspaper accounts and from the sometimes unreliable recollections of old-timers. The number and variety of the stories make it easy to ascertain that Jim was a hellion from the start. He could not stay out of trouble. Sober, he was given to wrong-doings which seemed to be little more than the deviations of a young man with wild oats to sow. Drunk, he exhibited a streak of killing meanness which could end fatally for friend or foe.

Gus Bequette, a grandson of pretty, spirited Mary Graves of Donner party fame, who spent much of his working life at the exciting and hazardous job of driving the horses that pulled Visalia's first steam powered pumper fire engine, put in his first day at school in 1883 at the old Outside Creek School south of Farmersville. His parents lived on a ranch, as Californians persist in calling anything from five to five thousand acres, and their neighbors were the McKinneys—Andrew having taken a lease on a large tract of grain land.

Ed McKinney was in one of the upper grades at the little one-room school. He escorted Gus to school that first day. Gus knew Ed's older brother, Jim, as a grown youth in his early twenties, and Gus had a little boy's admiration for Jim because he was patient with small boys and had a reputation as an expert horseman who broke colts for ranchers of the neighborhood and drove a long-line team in freighting lumber from the mountains. This skill he probably learned from his father, who had been a teamster in the mountainous country around Leadville. Jim hauled the lumber from which the Union school west of Farmersville was constructed. It took a driver who knew his business to bring a team and heavily laden wagon down the steep grades and around the sharp curves of the mountain roads.

Young Jim McKinney spent his Saturday nights and between-jobs leisure in the saloons and gambling halls of Visalia. Because drink aroused in him a sinister recklessness and because he was not the kind to truckle to anyone when he was in such condition, he was frequently in trouble. His bone-handled six-gun accompanied him everywhere, and from the stories his contemporaries tell, he soon began to carry a knife and brass knuckles as well.

One night he was in one of the fandango halls on the northern fringe of Visalia, dancing with a handsome Spanish girl whose figure was well rounded in the mode of the times. A jealous suitor for the girl's favors expressed a resentment of McKinney and made menac-

• 53

ing gestures in his direction, accompanied by insults. Jim, his temper edged by the load of liquor he was carrying, hauled out his six-shooter to let some daylight into the man who was pestering him and his companion. As he fired, the fandango girl jumped between them and the plump overhang of her posterior caught the bullet that was intended for Jim's rival, doubtlessly preventing her from practicing various aspects of her vocation for several days. Her screams prompted the belligerents to depart hastily before the wrath of her friends and the law descended, for violence to a woman was not acceptable even in the liberal code of the bar rooms of the Old West.

One beautiful, warm spring night the people of the Locust Grove "stringtown" along the creeks east of Farmersville gathered at their little schoolhouse for the annual show-off of the graduates before proud relatives. One of Jim's younger brothers had attended this school and had gotten into trouble with the teacher. Jim chose graduation night, while his mother was attending the program at the school, to demonstrate his protectiveness for his little brother against the disciplinary measures of the teacher. Fortifying himself with liquor, he appeared at the doorway of the school while the program was in full swing and began to hurl profanely emphatic challenges at the teacher. Someone slammed the door and locked him out, hoping to discourage him. McKinney fitted on his brass knuckles and let go a blow with his fist that split the door panel from top to bottom.

Walter Boggan, a deputy constable, and a number of other men jumped up and ran to the door to cope with the intruder. Although he was unarmed, Boggan took the lead. As he stepped into the darkness outside, Mc-Kinney struck at him with a knife and slashed the deputy deeply on the arm, effectively discouraging further attack. McKinney then fled into the darkness, shouting threats and curses and daring any man to follow him. None did.

On another occasion while he was living near Farmersville, Jim came into the sleepy little town one hot afternoon and imbibed a few shots of red-eye at the corner saloon. Later he joined a knot of loafers on a stack of lumber at the lumber yard behind the saloon, just across the street from the general store operated by T. J. Brundage.

A yellow cat started picking its way daintily across the street toward the store, stepping high and carefully to avoid sinking into the thick layer of dust. Jim drew his six-shooter and, unable to resist such a mincing target, directed several well aimed shots into the dust just under the cat. The reaction of the cat may be assumed, although its reaction is not mentioned in the incident as related by old-timers. Their account concerns the reaction of the usual knot of loafers on the porch of the store, the customers within, and the proprietor. The scamper for security from the ricocheting bullets which splattered into the board-and-batten store front caused considerable merriment among the loafers across the street in the lumber yard, and McKinney left the scene the hero of the hour.

• 55

It may be assumed from the tales told by his contemporaries that such incidents were commonplace with McKinney, and his life was just one scrape after another. He drifted around the valley, keeping just ahead of the tolerance, and managed to stay out of jail.

Always attracted to the most lively communities, he began hanging around the gambling halls of the booming town of Merced, 100 miles to the north of Visalia. In 1885 it was a comparatively new county seat community with a sea of rich grain land around it. It was to remain an island of vice in a sea of reform until the middle part of the next century.

In Merced McKinney took up with two ruffians of his own age and disposition, Robert Lee McFarlane and Alfred Hulse, who were to play an important part in his education as a badman and in his ultimate fate. McFarlane and Hulse had already made their reputations as gunmen and killers. One June night in 1884, this pair of hoodlums got into a fracas in a Portuguese dance hall and when the smoke cleared away one Antone Enos, a country boy fresh from the Azores who could not even speak English, lay dead upon the floor. Three of his companions were painfully wounded. McFarlane was placed under arrest, charged with murder, while his pal, Al Hulse, faced a lesser charge of assault with a deadly weapon.

The dance hall catered to and was patronized by Portuguese speaking people, and it seems unlikely that McFarlane and Hulse were there for any other purpose than to stir up a little fun among the naïve immigrants. The man who was slain and those who were wounded were sitting in the room devoted to dancing, near the piano to enjoy the music. The barroom was separated from the dance hall by an arched doorway. McFarlane came through the arch and left Hulse standing in it to cover him. Then he walked by the row of young Portuguese seated near the piano and began jeering and insulting them.

When resentment was exhibited, McFarlane drew his gun and fired at the one nearest to him. Hulse, too, opened up, and the Portuguese who could fled from the scene, leaving the two hoodlums triumphant.

In the trial proceedings, McFarlane claimed the Portuguese, Enos, had pulled a gun on him and he fired in self defense. Hulse, of course, corroborated his statement and said that he was forced to draw his gun and help to defend McFarlane.

No other witnesses were presented to show that Enos had a gun, and Enos' friends heartily denied that he possessed a weapon of any kind. Their stories, presented through the medium of an interpreter, could hardly expect to win the credence of the jury. It was seldom that "foreigners" who spoke with an accent or did not speak English at all received the same consideration in western justice as the person whose English was spoken with western or southern accent. The jury deadlocked, and the vote was such that the district attorney asked that the case be dismissed. McFarlane and Hulse went free.

McFarlane's next scrape with the law occurred within a few months, and this time his associate was Jim McKinney, a shooting scrape involving a bartender in

• 57

Snelling, the old county seat town east of Merced. This time McFarlane did not go free. He was found guilty of assault with a deadly weapon and was sentenced to Folsom prison for two years. McKinney was acquitted.

Within a few weeks, however, McKinney was back in court, charged with simple assault against the person of one John Gibbons of Merced Falls, a sawmill town on the Merced River east of Snelling. McKinney's reputation was such that the judge decided to discourage him from hanging around the county. He fined McKinney $500, a sizeable sum for those days.

Al Hulse drifted around the valley towns, gambling and tending bar. In 1892, he was involved in a shooting in a Merced saloon. Two men were seriously wounded, but both survived. Hulse was sentenced to prison on two charges of assault with a deadly weapon.

IV

$\mathbb{B}$ᴵʟʟʏ Cᴀʀᴅᴇʀ, the old faro dealer from Bodie, when asked if he had ever been in any trouble in that rugged mining town, was emphatic in his reply.

"Hell no! If a man minded his own business he could live in safety in the toughest of the mining boom towns, but if he wanted trouble, he didn't have to look very far to get it. I am here today because I learned early to mind my own business."

Peace officers of the Old West were sometimes closely identified with the gambling and saloon elements. Not infrequently popular bartenders and saloon keepers ran for the office of sheriff and won. A man dealing cards for a gambling house might turn up as a deputy. It was not unusual for men to hold down jobs in saloons and gambling halls while serving in the double role of deputy sheriff or marshal.

It was sometimes the practice of the saloon man and the professional gambler to profit from the earnings of prostitutes. Saloon proprietors might have nearby a convenient rooming house or crib with a bevy of girls under the direction of a madam. A gambler very likely had one favorite girl to whom he sent customers and whose earnings he shared. When luck ran bad, a broke gambler could always get a stake for a new start from a profitable prostitutional property. The lonely outcast woman who received her lord's friendship was steadfastly loyal and gladly shared her hard-earned money with him.

Not all saloon men stooped to taking profits from the fleshpots, however. One such man was Ed Fudge, who owned a saloon but was seldom in it, preferring to spend his active hours as a peace officer. He served both as deputy marshal of Visalia and as a deputy sheriff for the county. Ed was a taciturn old bachelor, well known for the quality of his courage. On one of the numerous occasions when it became desirable to take McKinney into custody, Fudge was detailed to go out to Farmersville and bring him in. Farmersville, six miles southeast of Visalia, was to become in the 1930s a refuge for fugitives from the Dust Bowl and midwestern farm mechanization, but in McKinney's day it was a peaceful crossroads settlement whose major extra-legal activity was the sale of liquor to the few sickly Indians who still camped along the nearby creek channels.

Fudge arrived in Farmersville by horse and buggy and made inquiry of the village blacksmith concerning McKinney. The smith, whose shop was located prominently near the main intersection, enabling him to keep a casual check on the comings and goings of most of the populace, told Fudge he had seen McKinney board a wheat wagon headed for Visalia, and the deputy must have passed him on the road.

Fudge turned his rig back toward Visalia and before long overtook a wagon with two men on the seat. He pulled up beside it and motioned the driver to stop his team. "You Jim McKinney?" he called to the man beside the driver.

"I sure am. Who wants me?" the man challenged.

"I do," said Fudge, and with these words lifted up a huge revolver which he had placed conveniently on the buggy seat beside him, pointing it squarely at McKinney. "I have a warrant for your arrest."

McKinney raised no ruckus, but he always resented Fudge's means of getting the drop on him, treating him as a criminal and a dangerous one at that. When this incident blew over, as it soon did, McKinney made his boast in public about what he would do next time Fudge was sent to arrest him. As Jim was never long out of trouble, the opportunity came soon. Fudge, again bearing a warrant for McKinney's arrest, met Jim on the street in Visalia. Fudge was armed but had not drawn his weapon when he accosted McKinney. In a flash of anger, McKinney drew his gun and pulled the trigger. The weapon misfired and Fudge, although he had plenty of justification for shooting McKinney down

• 61

in self defense as the traditional western marshal would have done, calmly disarmed him and took him into custody.

If all six-shooters had performed as badly as McKinney's, the West would have been won with far fewer killings. It was the first of at least three occasions on which Jim's weapon refused duty. Because of two of the failures he was tried for assault with a deadly weapon, when otherwise the charges would almost certainly have been murder, for his aim was deadly when his weapon performed as it should. Perhaps it was his bad experience with six-guns that caused him eventually to lose faith in them and turn to the shotgun.

In 1886 Andrew McKinney moved to Porterville, taking up a large acreage on a rental basis north of town. His son, Ed, became a popular bartender in Porterville and later a partner in a saloon. Jim was by this time committed to the dissolute life. He earned his living most of the time as a gambler, and he favored dice over cards. He had a woman with whom he consorted and for whom he procured. He worked occasionally as a teamster but occasionally hired out as a "shotgun man," or ditch guard, in the irrigation squabbles that continually broke out. He was considered to be quite a lady's man, and he was to become involved in one of the juicest scandals of the decade in Porterville.

The town was undergoing a period of expansion and prosperity. Laurence Barrett, a leading West Coast tragedian, thought sufficiently well of the little community to invest his money in a new hotel, the Pioneer, which was to be the valley's finest in its day. It still stands prominently on the city's main street, housing a modern drug store on its ground floor while the upper portion is still devoted to rented rooms.

Much of the news and many of the advertisements that went into O'Clancy's *Porterville Enterprise* came from the row of shoddy saloons in the two blocks north of Porter Slough, a water course which bisected the business district and periodically threatened to overflow and flood the town. Most of the saloons, if not exactly respectable, were quiet places and O'Clancy and his editor, Aubrey Lumley, the town physicians and other dignitaries frequently stepped in for a quiet dram at the close of the day's work. Others, however, were rough places in which fights were common occurrences and gun play so frequent that Lumley was moved to editorialize that "the gun must go" before the consequences became serious. His argument was entirely logical. There was a law against the carrying of concealed weapons, and Lumley made the point that if the law were enforced, the exhibition of weapons would be stopped.

The saloons were the center of much of the adult male activity of the community. Their owners had given them the friendly or imposing names that were common to saloons in the West. Frank Jersey operated a place he called the Reception. Jack Woodrough chose the name IXL, and Dave Mosier attempted to give his hole-in-the-wall greater status by calling it the Mint. When the Pioneer Hotel was completed, its oasis went under the name of the hotel. One modern name cropped up, the Electric Light, as it was one of the first

• 63

places in town to be lighted by electricity after the Pioneer Water Company installed an unreliable generator on the Tule River in 1889. The Exchange and the Palace saloons were prominent drink emporiums and advertised their more genteel atmosphere in the *Enterprise.*

Tom Simmons gave his place the name of Mountain Lion, as the big attraction was two live mountain lion cubs which were usually chained one on each side of the entrance. When the cubs became half grown, a favorite prank of frivolous drunks was to turn them loose on the town. It was great fun to watch some inebriate, staggering homeward at midnight, come face to face with two snarling, overgrown cats. Katie and Susie, as Tom called them, were wandering in the streets one night as a dignified pillar of the community was driving his wife home from a late social function. The horse encountered the two cats on a dark street and bolted in panic. Next day the citizen demanded that the lions be banished, threatening Tom with a lawsuit. Tom reluctantly parted with Katie and Susie, selling them to a traveling show. He made a clean sweep by also selling to the show a precocious parrot which had learned so well the explosive vocabulary of the muleskinners who patronized the saloon that the bird could not be trusted outside where ladies might pass by.

Topics for discussion over drinks in the saloons were varied and exciting in the late '80s and early '90s. Sam Whately had been murdered at Tailholt and his mortal remains had been buried before the sheriff was satisfied with his investigation. The coroner was instructed to

64 •

find, if he could, the bullet that killed Sam, that it might be compared and studied. The coroner exhumed the body and, lacking x-ray with which to locate the leaden slug, took what seemed to him to be the most expeditious method. He boiled the remains until the flesh fell from the bones, then probed in his grisley stew with the hope that the bullet might have become separated. Either he lacked the stomach to make a proper search or the bullet was not in the body, for it was not found.

Nick Wren, a deputy sheriff, had been murdered by a man he sought to arrest for wife beating. Johnny Crawford, whose name was to crop up in the McKinney story a dozen years later, had started a stage between Visalia and the new town of Exeter. Someone cut the Pioneer Water Company dam on the Tule River, blacking out Porterville as the electric generator ceased to function.

The Utopian socialists of the Kaweah Commonwealth colony on the Kaweah River were proposing to build a railroad into the Giant Forest and were accused of preparing to log off the magnificent stand of the world's oldest and largest trees, including that greatest of them all, General Sherman, which the colonists named after their own hero, Karl Marx. Professor Shook had just completed digging a well eight feet in diameter on his property near Porterville and had the crazy notion of pumping irrigation water from it. Constable Rose decided to try out the *Enterprise's* suggestion that the law against the carrying of firearms be enforced. He arrested a saloon proprietor for keeping a disorderly house because he permitted gunplay. The trial was held

• 65

on a very warm day. The jury brought in a verdict of acquittal in record time and adjourned to the nearest saloon for a cooling draught.

The lusty humor of the saloon crowd was exhibited in a practical joke directed against a young Porterville man who had been deputized as a deputy sheriff, thereby enhancing his already inflated estimation of his charm with the ladies. The cronies who hung out at one of the saloons decided to puncture his ego. They selected as bait a fair-skinned young man who wasn't too well known around town. They gave the young man a close shave, rigged him out in feminine frills, and presented him to the deputy as a blind date. The deputy strutted to the nearest confectionery store with his bogus sweetie. As he sat prominently near the window, sipping soda and endeavoring to overcome the "maiden's" shyness, he suddenly became aware of a crowd of leering, laughing men gathered outside, making lewd and suggestive gestures. The temporary transvestite across the table could no longer conceal his true identity. Next day, the young deputy turned in his star and pointed his red face for parts unknown.

The McKinneys were much in the news. Ed and a man named Wheeler formed a partnership and bought the Bank Exchange Saloon, which featured an assertive brand of whiskey aptly labeled Davy Crockett. The *Enterprise* reported that Mother McKinney had left for Canada for an extended visit.

Jim made news of another sort.

He got drunk one night and started a rumpus in a saloon. A deputy constable was called to restore peace

and tried to calm the raging trouble-maker with sooth-
ing words and supplications. McKinney cursed the
deputy, slapped his face, and threatened him with
worse if he did not leave him alone. The deputy left
without making an arrest and also without talking Mc-
Kinney into going home.

The *Enterprise* was at the time whipping up its appeal for civic reform and, learning of the incident between McKinney and the deputy constable, editorially
demanded to know why such an indignity to the seren-
ity of Porterville should be tolerated. In biting language
the editor recommended that men be deputized as
peace officers who had the courage to enforce the law.
It was the old familiar plea made many times by men
of honor and decency in the Old West—a plea which
often went unheeded because men of courage were not
common.

If Aubrey Lumley was the *Enterprise* writer who
prepared the editorial, then there was no hypocrisy in
it. Lumley was a cultured, eastern-bred gentleman
whose clean collars and careful dress were out of place
in dusty little Porterville. While his sartorial elegance
may have typed him as a dude, Lumley was sufficiently
rugged physically to hold his own in tough company.
He was a big man, and somewhere in the course of his
classic education he had been taught the manly art of
self-defense, an asset which helped to put grit into his
editorial columns. Years later, Lumley was to make
rough-and-tumble fist-fight history in Porterville in a
celebrated clash with a doughty Irish priest over politi-
cal differences. Father Farrelley spoke vigorously from

• 67

his pulpit on various aspects of public affairs and Lumley, a staunch Mason, went to listen. In his editorial columns he denounced the Irishman's advocacies with vehemence and skill, with the result that the priest threatened to make him eat his words. Lumley took up the challenge, and one day the two men met on a downtown street. Words were exchanged, and soon the two husky men were trading blows. Both had physical courage to match that of their convictions, and both had stamina. The battle raged for more than an hour over most of two blocks of the business district while men, women and children flocked in from all parts of town to give moral support to their favorite. When the fight finally ended from the sheer exhaustion of the combatants, Lumley's partisans rushed him into the Pioneer Hotel to lave his bruised and bleeding face. Both the Mason and the Catholic were spirited out of town by their respective factions for fear of reprisal. After tempers had cooled down, each returned to town with a convincing respect for the courage and tenacity of his opponent.

McKinney's reputation might have been sufficient to frighten a small town constable, but Editor Lumley was not to be intimidated. He continued to stop in for his evening dram at the Mountain Lion Saloon, and on one of these occasions he found McKinney lounging by the pot-bellied stove in the corner, irritable with drink. McKinney spotted his detractor and began hurling threats and curses at him. Lumley was no man to take abuse, and he approached the badman. McKinney drew his gun, took careful aim, and squeezed the trigger. The

68 •

gun missed fire. Lumley was on Jim before the gunman could spin the chamber, and with a great blow of his fist flattened the terror of Skidrow on the floor of the saloon. Lumley disarmed the fallen man and went back to the bar to finish his drink. He drank alone, for the rest of the customers had vanished through the exits at the first suggestion of trouble.

Early in August of 1889 the readers of the *Enterprise* were diverted by the report of a legal action instituted in the court of Justice of the Peace Robert Redd. A prominent rancher, who for the purposes of pseudo-nymity in protection of possible descendants shall here be called Jasper, filed suit against McKinney, charging him with obtaining money under false pretenses.

The circumstances were stated completely in the *Enterprise*, and the spicy reading helped to ease the monotony of the summer heat for Porterville. Jasper alleged that Julia, to use another fictitious name, the young wife of a man who worked for Jasper on his ranch, had left her two young daughters with her mother at the 18-Mile-House, an inn and tavern on the stage road north of Porterville, and had gone off to San Francisco, presumably in search of medical treatment for an illness. While she was in the city, Julia wired Jasper for the loan of $100, which Jasper sent without question, as he was a kindly individual.

However, word reached Jasper, by what means the *Enterprise* did not disclose, that Julia, far from being physically incapacitated, was seen cavorting in the night spots of the Barbary Coast with the notorious Jim McKinney. Jasper was furious, assuming that the young woman had gone off to the city in company with the dashing gunman to escape the humdrum life in the country. McKinney showed up in Porterville before Julia returned, and Jasper took legal means to make McKinney the scapegoat for causing Jasper to look like an easy mark.

It proved to be an action that Jasper made in haste to be repented at leisure. The rancher found himself in a bad situation. When it came time for McKinney's arraignment, Billy Rose, the constable, brought the badman into court. Also subpoenaed had been Julia's lawful wedded husband, who presumably was to testify for the plaintiff. But neither Jasper nor Julia's husband showed up for the arraignment. The scandal had brought a large number of spectators into court to view the proceedings, and Judge Redd was not to let them down. He tossed the case against McKinney out of court, but before doing so had Jasper and Julia's husband brought in on a bench warrant, and he fined Jasper $50 and the husband $25 for failure to obey the summons. Next day, Jasper filed suit against Julia.

Julia arrived back in Porterville thoroughly contrite, repentant, but not subdued. She was to pay the piper more dearly than she knew, and already retribution had dealt her a nasty blow. While she was kicking up her heels, if such she did, on old Pacific Street, both her daughters were stricken with diphtheria at their grandmother's home. The family had tried frantically and futilely to find Julia. The youngest child died without benefit of the consoling caresses of her mother. Perhaps it was this that made Jasper so vengeful.

By the time her case came up in court, Julia obviously thought she had been punished enough, and she had made her peace with her conscience sufficiently to face her accuser with pride and defiance. The *Enterprise* reporter watched her conduct with a mixture of sympathy and healthy male interest, for he was to report that she appeared "very attractive" as she took the witness stand.

Her defense was simple and effective. She looked Jasper squarely in the eye, then turned to Judge Redd and told him firmly that the loan for which she had bargained with Jasper was a valid one. She had promised to pay it back by cooking at the ranch.

"She said she would do it if it took five years, she told the judge with a proud toss of her shapely head," reported the *Enterprise.*

Against such a combination of charm and pathos, Jasper's case fell apart. Judge Redd dismissed the charges.

Julia went back to her husband, contrite and forgiven, despite the fact that it proved to be him who initiated the investigation which eventually alleged her to be shacked up with McKinney in the big city. They were not again separated until death took them many years later. They and the daughter who died so forlornly lie in eternal sleep not far from the grave of Jim McKinney. If Julia did not sleep with Jim in life as her enemies intimated, she was to lie not far from his side in death, with her husband safely between.

Jasper had not heard the legal last of the incident. McKinney hired himself an attorney with the imposing name of J. Oregon Sanders and filed suit for $5,000

• 71

against the rancher, charging him with false arrest. The case never came to court, possibly because of an out-of-court settlement but more probably because Sanders found that arrest could have scarcely caused $5,000 worth of inconvenience to his client, and certainly nothing could have damaged McKinney's reputation five cents worth at that stage of his life.

Late in the summer, while Mrs. McKinney was still visiting in Canada, hard-working Andrew McKinney was spared further anguish by the misdeeds of his devious son. He dropped dead of a heart attack at the age of sixty-one. Mrs. McKinney hurried home in time to sob a last farewell before his body was lowered into the grave, and the *Enterprise* gave his obituary the front page prominence the much respected man deserved.

"As the funeral service was read over the grave," solemnly reported the *Enterprise*, "Mrs. McKinney's grief brought tears to the eyes of many spectators. She was consoled by her sons, Matt, Ed, Jim and Jake."

Trouble did not abandon the funeral procession at the grave. On the way back from the cemetery Grey Eagle, the spirited horse of Jack Woodrough, the purveyor of spirits at the IXL Saloon, took fright and ran away, tossing Jack out onto the rough road. He was battered so badly he was unable to dispense his refreshments for several days.

V

MRS. McKINNEY, grieving for Andrew, was given short respite from her tribulations. Her eldest son, who was to express his devotion to his mother on numerous occasions even while in the process of wringing her heart with his misdeeds, was about to give her more cause for concern than he had in the past.

Now firmly established as Porterville's leading saloon row character, he had arrived at the termination of the toleration of the community—despite his ability to charm with his personality those whom he did not offend. The country was filling up with respectable people who were fed up with the excuse that brawling, gunplay and vice were just the simple sins of growing pains in western small towns. Porterville was surfeited with the nightly wrangles, the drunkenness, and with the gambling, pimping wild bunch in general. The *Enterprise's* campaign for reform was rising to a crescendo. During the fall of the year after the death of his father, McKinney was guzzling one night in the Reception Saloon and, over-stepping his capacity, slipped into one of his nasty moods. He began plaguing the customers and "generally raising hell," as the bartender, Tap Carter, was later to state in a complaint lodged against McKinney. Carter, one of the proprietors of the saloon, asked McKinney to leave. Instead of heeding the request, Jim hauled from his belt his Smith & Wesson .44 and pointed it at Carter. As the saloon man ducked behind the bar to go for his own weapon, the customers dived under tables or stampeded for exits.

Carter stuck his head up over the bar to check the position of his enemy. Jim aimed his gun and pulled the trigger. Instead of splitting the smoky, alcoholic air of the saloon with a roar and a burst of flame, the weapon merely snapped. Again McKinney was saved from committing murder by the timely prudence of his weapon in missing fire.

The foregoing facts are stated in the complaint of assault with a deadly weapon which Carter swore out against McKinney the next day, but some exciting details are lost to history. The files of the *Enterprise* terminate at this point, for in later years the office of this doughty old country journal burned. The files, except for two volumes Mr. Lumley happened to have at his home, were destroyed. As the transcripts of the trials have either been destroyed or are buried in the musty

74 •

rubble of courthouse accumulations, only the barest of legal proceedings stand documented in the files of the county clerk.

Carter and his friends must have had a busy time getting McKinney to leave the place, or perhaps Carter, as McKinney intimated later, got the drop on him and frightened him out. It is also likely that Jim gave Deputy Sheriff Lee O. Wren, a fearless peace officer, some trouble when he went to arrest him, for as a companion complaint to that of Carter, action was brought by Wren against Porterville's bad boy on an identical charge of assault with a deadly weapon.

Arraigned before Justice of the Peace Redd, McKinney was freed on bail furnished by Thomas McIntyre, one of his best friends; W. S. Henrahan, J. T. Simmons, and, of all people, M. J. O'Clancy, publisher of the *Enterprise* which so militantly campaigned against McKinney's kind.

At the preliminary hearing, McKinney sought to obtain a dismissal of the charge Carter had lodged against him on the grounds that Carter was armed and threatened him, and that McKinney had acted in self-defense in fear of his own life. It was a plea that had stood many a western badman in good stead in similar situations. Judge Redd would not consider it and ordered the badman held without bail in the county jail in Visalia.

Notwithstanding Judge Redd's action, McKinney's friends thought the charges against him were bolstered by flimsy evidence, and they believed he would easily win acquittal if tried in the superior court. Because of this common opinion, Jim's friends were shocked when

• 75

they heard that McKinney and his old friend, Robert McFarlane, had broken out of the county jail and escaped.

The jail was located on the ground floor of the courthouse, a customary architectural feature of many cow county courthouses of the day. The jail consisted of massive granite walls with barred windows and doors, a long corridor which served as a medium security section or "drunk tank," and a series of iron ceilinged cells for maximum security. The ceiling over the drunk tank was only plaster, and there was a space between the iron tops of the maximum security cells and the ceiling.

As prisoners of some prestige and because no one believed they would be so foolish as to try to escape when it was very likely they would beat the charges. McKinney and McFarlane were allowed the run of the drunk tank. Here they had access to the windows leading outside. They conversed at their own pleasure through the bars with their friends outside, and because of the popularity of the two among the saloon element, visitors were numerous. The *Visalia Times* suggested after the escape that the temptation "was made too easy to resist." A woman was seen talking to them and a short time later a man wearing a brown suit was seen to slip something through the bars to them. These things were reported, of course, only after the jailbirds had flown. Jim's friends said in later years that the woman was his girl friend of the moment and it was she who delivered the proper tools for the escape.

The tools they obtained consisted of a brace and bit. In the night they climbed to the top of one of the iron

cages and drilled a series of holes, spaced closely together, through the plaster and through the wood floor
of the county recorder's office just above. It was a simple matter to break out the circle thus encompassed,
ease themselves into the office above, and quietly make
their way out of the courthouse to freedom. As it turned
out, whoever had passed the tools for the break had
done them no favor, for the sheriff, Dan Overall, was a
man of conscience and the ability to defend it. He was
greatly incensed at the offense to his hospitality and
spared no pains to bring the fugitives back to the fold.

Someone saw to it that a pair of fast horses awaited
McKinney and McFarlane once they were outside, and
they fled northward into the darkness. Next day the
sheriff took their trail and traced it as far as Merced, a
hundred miles away, but there he learned that further
pursuit on horseback was fruitless. The two had hopped
a freight train and were far out of reach.

McKinney, having cleverly put one over on the
shrewd sheriff, could not resist adding insult to the injury he had caused to Overall's reputation as a sheriff.
Jim reached the haven of Cheyenne, Wyoming, where
a man of his habits might find many kindred souls. It
was the stamping ground of the Wild Bunch, as notorious a gang of outlaws as the West ever produced.
Whether McKinney sought to become a recruit in the
band is not known, but the possibility of his becoming
allied with them was eliminated when he sat down and
penned a letter to his old friend, Thomas McIntyre, in
Porterville.

"Dear Sir," he wrote formally. "I will drop you a few lines to let you know we have traded overcoats. I am going to start to Canada tomorrow. If they catch me I will keep them guessing. The snow is two feet deep here and still snowing. Give my friends regards and tell my enemies to .... Yours Respectfully, Jim McKinney."

In some manner the *Porterville Enterprise* obtained possession of the content of the letter and spread it in the columns. Sheriff Overall took it as a personal insult. Ordinarily he would have considered McKinney's flight to Wyoming a blessing, a good riddance to Tulare County of a citizen who had caused it nothing but trouble, and a savings to the taxpaying public of court and jail costs. But Sheriff Overall told his friends that he considered the letter to McIntyre a dig at his ability and he resolved to teach the outlaw a lesson. He wired Wyoming authorities to arrest and hold McKinney. By the time peace officers in Wyoming could act, McKinney had moved to Rawlins, and it was there that he was taken into custody and held. With extradition papers in order, Sheriff Overall left for Wyoming "with his grip full of bracelets," as the *Visalia Times* expressed it, indicating he would take no chances on his prisoner making a second escape.

Late in January the *Times* reported that Overall and McKinney were being forced to lay over in Reno because Donner Summit, over which the railroad crosses the Sierra, was snowbound. The *Times* reporter pouted that Overall wasn't giving out much information on the time of his expected arrival in Visalia and complained

that the press should be kept better informed, as Mc-
Kinney's escapades were the major news interest of the
day. However, there was justification for Overall's inclination to be close-mouthed. There was widespread
talk that Jim's brothers and friends were planning to
deliver him from custody by force when Overall arrived
with his prisoner in Visalia. Overall, knowing the
powerful effect of McKinney's magnetic personality on
his friends, realized it would not be inconceivable for
them to take such a risk. He was not taking any chances
on losing his prisoner again.

Moreover, McFarlane was still at large and was a
desperate enough character to organize a violent de-
livery. He had not followed McKinney to Wyoming
and was believed to be in hiding in the mountains east
of Merced.

While the pass between Reno and California was
having too much snow, Visalia and the mountains to
the east were having too much rain. High water in Visalia pushed the McKinney story off the front page of
the *Visalia Times* until the sheriff and his prisoner arrived, pale and drawn, in Visalia two weeks later, early
in February. With McKinney safely behind the double
security of one of the maximum security cells, with an
iron ceiling over his head and no access to windows
through which he might receive aid from his friends,
Overall was willing to discuss his trip.

It had not been a pleasant one. Overall and his prisoner had been stranded in Reno for fourteen days, and
Reno was then far from being the glittering amusement
center it was to become half a century later. McKinney

• 79

had been impounded in the calaboose, where he at once became ill with what his generation called "la grippe." Overall, too, came down with the malady and instead of being able to enjoy two weeks of enforced idleness at the expense of the county in which he was sheriff, he spent his time in bed, filled with aches, pains and sniffles. He arrived in Visalia 20 pounds lighter than when he left.

The law, with as unstable a prisoner as McKinney in custody and his friends from the tenderloins of Visalia and Porterville maneuvering uneasily outside in an effort to find a way to spring him, decided to waste as little time as possible processing him through court. Within a day or two he was arraigned before Superior Judge Cross on two counts of assault with a deadly weapon involving his quarrels with Tap Carter and Deputy Lee Wren plus a new serious count of jail breaking. For good measure, District Attorney W. R. Jacobs dug up an old charge of assault with intent to commit great bodily harm allegedly committed four years before against the person of Ed Fudge, but this charge was later dropped.

Acting as his own attorney, McKinney attempted to prove self-defense in the complaint of Carter. He sought to subpoena Frank Jersey, a partner of Carter in the saloon, but Jersey begged off on the grounds that he was too ill to go to court. Before the jury was impaneled to try him, Jim made a strong case of Carter's degree of blame for the quarrel, and the jury, after eight hours of debate, discarded the felony charge of assault with a deadly weapon in favor of a misdemeanor charge of simple assault, and brought in a verdict of guilty to the milder charge.

After hearing Wren's testimony on the second charge, the jury was out just long enough to grab a smoke before returning a verdict of guilty to assault with a deadly weapon on the person of Wren. A few days later, McKinney was tried for jail break, his only defense being that he felt he would not be treated fairly if he remained in jail to stand trial, a line of reasoning which could only prove offensive to the jury. It found him guilty on a single ballot.

With the grim prospect of prison before him, McKinney renewed his fight. He moved for a new trial, but Judge Cross cut him short. On March 10, McKinney was ordered into court for sentencing. For breaking jail Jim received the full penalty of the law, five years in prison, from the wrathful judge. Two more years were added for the assault on Deputy Wren, plus 90 days in the Tulare county jail on the charge of simple assault, plus a $500 fine. It was quite apparent that Judge Cross intended to make an example of Jim McKinney. Righteous folk who felt the brash young man had been allowed to go too long without paying for his misdeeds had no reason to complain of the penalty.

The severity of the sentence did not repress the arrogance of McKinney. "He smiled and almost laughed aloud as Judge Cross pronounced sentence in the case," the *Times* reported. "He left the courtroom smoking a cigar."

Back in his cell, he tried for an appeal to the state supreme court, but it was turned down. He was shipped

• 81

off to San Quentin to serve his time, and for the next several years Jim McKinney was off the front pages of the valley newspapers. In the interim, the public was to be well entertained by those Prodigal Sons, Chris Evans, John Sontag, and Ed Morrell, through the early part of the 19th century's last decade. McKinney, last of the western badmen, was to be off-stage for a while.

"The general public is well satisfied with the case as it is," said the *Times* in writing him off. "It believes Mc-Kinney got his just desserts."

VI

FROM HIS entry into San Quentin in 1899 until he broke into the grim society of known killers in Bakersfield in 1901 there is a hiatus of biographical information concerning the outlaw. He worked as a baker in the Big House, and in the absence of booze there is no doubt his ability to win friends should have given him standing among prisoners and guards. His mother and brothers visited him regularly, and there is no reason to believe he was anything but a model prisoner.

With time off for good behavior, it is likely that Mc-Kinney was out of prison by 1895 or 1896, and it is probable that he lived in San Francisco immediately following his release. One of the few copies of the *Porterville Enterprise* saved from those years related that

• 83

Mrs. McKinney was on an extended visit to San Francisco, and it is more than likely that she must have been with her favorite son, Jim. His friends of post-prison days said he had picked up a knowledge of the Chinese language, and it was their understanding that he had learned it in San Francisco's Chinatown. What he did, how or where he lived in the two or three years immediately following his release from prison, none of his friends recall.

One thing is certain: when he returned to the San Joaquin Valley he was a hardened badman nearing middle age, devoid of conscience or morals, as mature in vice and disrespect for the law as a term in prison could make him. If he had ever intended to go straight, the intention was soon to be eliminated by the temptations he found on his return to his old haunts and habits. He retained the winning personality and personal charm that created loyal and staunch supporters among his acquaintances, but he could handle liquor no better than he could in his youth. It depressed him, bringing to him a sinister, defensive mood from which he would lash out at friend or foe. Like a coiled rattlesnake, he was ready to strike at anything or anyone.

In the absence of newspaper files of Porterville in this period of the late 1890s, it is necessary to rely almost entirely on the memories of old men for the story of McKinney during this period. Their recollections, while perhaps inaccurate in detail and colored by the patina of hero worship the passing years have added, indicate that prison had done nothing for his moral rehabilitation.

Chester Doyle was among those close to McKinney in the late 1890s. His father, J. J. Doyle, one of the principals in the famed Mussel Slough tragedy in nearby Kings County in 1880 in which eight men lost their lives in a futile and unnecessary fight which grew out of a dispute between settlers and the railroad over land titles, alternately ran a summer resort at Mountain Home in the nearby Sierra Nevada and a rooming house at Main and Putnam streets in Porterville. It was at the Doyle rooming house in Porterville that McKinney made his official residence on his return.

"He was as fine a friend as a boy could have when he wasn't drinking," said Doyle, following the pattern of other testimonials to the badman.

"His room was right across the hall from mine, and I saw him nearly every day. One night he got drunk and got in a quarrel with John McFarland in a saloon. After considerable bickering, McKinney took a shot at John.

"Jim ran for the rooming house and shot out the street light on the corner before he came up the stairs. He woke up my father and told him to get everyone out of the rooming house, as there was going to be the damnedest gun battle Porterville ever saw and he didn't want any of his friends to get hurt.

"Dad cleared the place and then went down and hunted up Constable Sigler, who was raising a force of deputies to go after McKinney. Dad told the constable just to let Jim alone until he sobered up, that he would calm dawn and would listen to reason.

"Sigler took my father's advice, and sure enough, by morning McKinney was over his fit of temper and was sorry he had caused trouble. McFarland refused to press charges and Jim was not arrested.

"I am certain that had the constable tried to lead his men up those rooming house stairs after McKinney, there would have been killings, for McKinney told us he planned to lie down on the hall floor and sweep the head of the stairs with gunfire if anyone tried to come up."

Another incident in the post-prison life of McKinney comes from Jay Brown, who heard his father relate it. Struggles over the feeble flow of the Tule River continued, and Jim and Ed McKinney hired out as "shotgun men" to guard the brush dam the Pioneer Water Company had thrown across the river. A hastily organized vigilante company of downstream farmers whose crops were withering for lack of irrigation water hastened to the spot and took positions behind trees and bushes near the dam.

Their spokesman stepped courageously forward and informed the McKinneys that they had come for the purpose of blowing up the dam. Ed McKinney raised his shotgun and declared he would blow the head off the first man to try it, whereupon the bold captain of the vigilantes, courting martyrdom, declared his intention of trying. If Ed McKinney blew his head off, well and good, but with a sweep of his arm to indicate the numerous gun barrels protruding from behind trees and through the foliage, the leader said the others would not only blow up the dam, but the McKinneys with it.

Ed McKinney quickly and without rancor adjusted his attitude to fit the reality: "Well," he said, "I was hired to guard the dam, but I am not being paid to get myself killed. Go ahead, boys, blow 'er up!" And he and his brother Jim shouldered their guns and left the spot.

Doyle's reminiscences concerning Jim McKinney in that era concern his conduct of a little tent saloon near one of the lumber camps near the Doyle resort at Mountain Home. A bunch of the teamsters and loggers were drinking there one evening and decided that, as the stock of the temporary business was not very large, they could cut the cost of their pleasure by purchasing the business outright

After much good-natured bargaining, McKinney and his customers settled on a price of $150. The deal was consummated, and McKinney stepped out from behind the bar and took his place as a customer, while one of the new owners tied on the bartender's apron and proceeded to serve drinks on the house in celebration of the grand opening under new ownership. The business was quickly liquidated.

Scotty's Chop House, located in the middle of Porterville's saloon row, was a working man's eating and drinking establishment that remained open 24 hours a day, month in and month out, without holidays.

"We didn't even have a lock for the front door," recalled Webb Loyd, who was for many years a partner in the operation and also cooked there during the years that Jim McKinney was a good customer.

"One time a prominent man died and we wanted to close the chop house during the funeral. We had to go

• 87

out and find some boards to nail over the door," said Loyd.

Art Kilbreth, another of the cooks at Scotty's, was a friend of McKinney and in later years was to recall that the badman was a favored customer with the help because of his quiet courtesy.

McKinney spent a great deal of time as a gambler in Dave Moshier's Mint Saloon, across the street from the chop house. Occasionally he tended bar there as well. These occupations, along with an occasional job as a "shotgun man," were his chief sources of income.

However, it is also more than likely that during this period of his life he did as many other gamblers did; he became associated with a prostitute, procuring for her as well as sharing in her earnings. The person who became known as "McKinney's girl" shall for the purposes of this narrative, on the off-chance that she may still be alive and a respected great-grandmother, be known fictitiously as Sarah. This woman is well remembered among men of an age no longer much concerned with sex. Apparently she became more than just a chattel to McKinney, for he spent much time with her and was extremely jealous of her; it was a strange relationship of procurer-and-prostitute, man-and-mistress; it was said that McKinney suffered no man to make passes at his girl except in a strictly business way.

Sarah, in the memories of men who solemnly state that they visited her for purely social reasons or on legitimate errands of one kind or another, was a most unusual personality for one in her profession. She was well educated and kept her room full of excellent books,

88 •

including many classics, which she read between entertainments, and perhaps during. She was a small person, pretty, and a good conversationalist, readily adapting herself to all masculine types and equally pleasing to the rough teamster or the cultured professional man.

The curious who asked how a woman of such obvious education, charm and intellect had come to descend to such a life were told that she came from a good eastern family and had been a school teacher in Connecticut. She had fallen for the suave line of an army officer who was full of romance, passion, and promises, but turned out to be already married. After her disgrace, Sarah fled west to seek her fortune in a less circumscribed field than education.

This "cute little trick," as one man described her fifty-five years after his last visit to her house, was the most desired of the scarlet women who infested the red-light district which took up a block on Oak Street about two blocks east of Porterville's Main Street. She got her professional start in Porterville as one of the girls who worked for the town's most popular madam, whose business thrived unhindered for many years and who is remembered with affection as a fixture of the early days. Lest she, too, holds a better place in the memory of someone who knew not her true calling, her identity will be cloaked in this volume behind the name of Lottie.

After Jim McKinney took up with Sarah, the two could see no reason why Sarah should share her prestige and profits with Lottie and Jim set her up in a little house of her own across the block from Lottie's place,

• 89

only a couple of blocks from where the widowed Mother McKinney lived. Jim was to spend much of his time with Sarah and it was she who was to have custody of his prized personal possessions, including his guns.

"It always seemed to me," mused one old-timer who had made the rounds as a young man, "that there was an unusually large number of ex-school teachers in the redlight districts, arriving there for much the same reason as Sarah. I suppose, at that, it was not a much worse life than fighting the rough and rowdy kids who attended those pioneer schools and certainly opportunities for marriage were just about equal in both professions."

While McKinney's prestige was considerable in the element with which he consorted, there were others in Porterville besides Aubrey Lumley who did not truckle to him. Billy Maston, whose days as a policeman in Porterville followed the McKinney era, recalled that another such person was Hy Williams, a bartender with a temper as quick as McKinney's.

Jim got drunk in a saloon in which Williams was tending bar one night and began raising a rumpus. Hy took about all he could stand and told Jim either to quiet down or leave. McKinney, hurling epithets at Hy, started toward him with his right hand moving for the gun that was stuck in his belt. Hy reached for the back-bar and gathered up a handful of beer schooners which he began pitching at the drunken gunman.

McKinney's wrath wilted. He was too busy ducking to shoot. Hy not only drove him out the door, but chased

him two blocks down the street, firing his beer mugs
as often as he could get within range.

McKinney did not spend all his time in Porterville.
When Bakersfield began booming under the impetus
of the sensational Kern River oil strike, there was plenty
of money for an unscrupulous gambler to gather from
the gullible oil field roustabouts, and plenty of entertainment in Bakersfield's seamy tenderloin to accom-
modate the most catholic taste. It was there that James
McKinney was to win officially the full notoriety of
man-killer.

There is legend a-plenty that McKinney had killed
before the Bakersfield incident, but there is no historical
evidence to corroborate the stories which have grown
up. It was known that he was in "bad trouble" in Leadville, but his mother's account of the incident indicates
it was not murder. One of his friends had heard that he
had been involved in a killing in San Francisco and for
that reason fled the city to return to Porterville following his release from prison. Certainly it is not inconceivable that he could have killed once or more times,
for there are many unsolved murders on record in the
Old West for which someone was responsible, and Mc-
Kinney was not above cold blooded murder, as he was
to demonstrate when the occasion demanded.

For the record, he killed his first man on the morning
of Friday, December 13, 1901, in a stinking alley in the
Bakersfield tenderloin when a bullet from his gun found
the heart of his ruffian friend, Thomas Sears, better
known among the drunks, gamblers, and dance hall
girls of Bakersfield as "Long Red."

● 91

It was the only one of six killings in which McKinney was to be involved in which his primary weapon was not the shotgun, and it was the only one which was not on Sunday. Friday the 13th was to be Red Sears' unlucky day.

Red, who was Missouri born, was about ten years younger than Jim. A big, rough man with a great torch of flaming red hair, he was quick and powerful with his fists. He had a bad record as a brawler in Visalia and other towns where he had practiced his trade as a gambler. McKinney, naturally, had encountered him in the saloons and gambling halls of valley towns from Merced to Porterville, and when they found themselves in Bakersfield at the same time, their friendship was such that they took a room together. They made a strange pair. Sears was loud and blustering, coarse in appearance, a boasting bully of a man. McKinney was quiet, neat in appearance, and except when drinking deported himself with almost courtly demeanor.

There are those alive as this is written who firmly believe that the Sears killing was a premeditated plot on the part of Sears' enemies to get rid of him; they do not imply, however, that McKinney was hired to do the job, only that the two were thrown together in a drinking spree in hopes that Sears would provoke McKinney into a killing mood. If there was such a scheme, it worked very well indeed, but looking at the evidence from the perspective of more than half a century it seems unlikely that the killing was planned. There can be little doubt, however, that the powers of the tenderloin were so pleased with the results that they took some pains to see that McKinney did not suffer for his act. Red Sears had bullied and threatened a good many men in Bakersfield, and they were not the kind of men who could take such treatment passively.

There is no better place to get a picture of violent death than from the transcript of the old-fashioned coroner's inquest. It was the custom for the coroner to line up six men as a jury as soon as possible after the death to be investigated and to present them with the evidence. It was the coroner's jury's job to determine how the deceased arrived at that state and the assumption was that the district attorney could take his cue from the decision as to whether someone or something was to blame besides the deceased or an act of God. Modern society, squeamish in the presence of death, has almost made the word itself forbidden in polite company and the colorful coroner's inquest of the past has disappeared, along with the wake and the lowering of the coffin into the grave in the presence of the anguished family.

The old-time inquest was held within a day or two after the death, often with the unburied body near at hand to be viewed and to lend reality. The memories of the witnesses were still fresh and their emotions unsalved by retrospect. Those involved had not yet had time to figure out the ultimate consequences, and testimony was more poignant than that which was given at trials many weeks after the death.

It is certain that the many witnesses who gave testimony at the inquest into the death of Thomas Sears on December 17, four days after Sears was shot, viewed the events very differently. Some saw it as justifiable homicide by McKinney in self defense. Others were equally sure it was a cold blooded murder of a man who had deliberately disarmed himself. Fortunately for Mc-Kinney, either by chance or by arrangement, those who saw it the latter way and so testified at the inquest could not be found by the sheriff when he later subpoenaed them as witnesses for the trial.

At the inquest, Coroner Frank Buckreus swore himself in as the first witness and launched the proceedings with a few gruesome technical facts. On the morning of December 13 he had been called to the alley between 19th and 20th Streets at the rear of Charles Cohn's general merchandise store. There he found the body of Thomas Sears, flat on its back, arms extended, and to use the coroner's own words, "dead as a hammer."

Sears' coat was unbuttoned and there was a neat bullet hole through his waistcoat as well as through the white muslin shirt underneath. The hole extended into the skin four inches below the left nipple, two inches to the left of the median line. As Dr. A. J. Shafer, the next witness was to testify, it was as neat a heart shot as a man bent on killing might hope to make. The left ventricle was quite smashed, and from it Dr. Shafer, while performing the autopsy, had removed a heavy bullet as well as part of the paper wadding from the cartridge.

The inquest was well attended, and Coroner Buckreus had several star performers for his show, as it was a well witnessed killing. One who could speak with considerable authority was Deputy Sheriff John Crawford. He was occupied with a personal matter in the outhouse near the alley at the time of and within a few feet of the fatal shooting. J. J. Carey and Warren McDonald were also on the scene, for they had been carousing with the killer and his victim, but by their own admissions their minds were so immersed in alcohol at the time that the whole affair seemed to them like a dim and unrealistic nightmare.

Another important witness who claimed to have been stone sober and to have witnessed every detail from an exceptional vantage point was W. H. Meachem, who said he was a hack driver. It was he who told the story that McKinney had cause to fear.

In addition to those above, Buckreus was to introduce several others whose testimony only added confusion to the general picture given to the jury.

Deputy Crawford, after being duly sworn as a witness, told of sitting in the outhouse near the alley "when I heard some jawing going on just outside." He peered through the lattice work which helped to lend privacy to the privy's interior and was able to see Sears in the alley, but his view was so limited by the structure of the outhouse door and lattice that he could not see McKinney, with whom he assumed Sears was arguing. Johnny testified that he saw Sears draw his six-shooter from his belt, and as Sears raised the weapon, the deputy grabbed up his pants and jumped outside.

He heard, but did not see, the fatal shot fired.

"McKinney had his gun like this," Crawford told the jury, making the gesture of a man aiming a gun at someone, "and Sears was falling."

"I says to him, 'What's the matter, Jim?' and he said 'He can't (obscenity) me.' I says, 'You'll have to submit to arrest,' and he says, 'I'll go with you, but I want to keep my gun until I get to jail.' I said, 'All right, come back until I get mine.' "

Crawford then described how he picked up Sears' gun, not mentioning in what position or how far from the body it was lying. Then, he said, he went back into the toilet and retrieved his own gun from the box in which he had placed it; then he and McKinney went off to jail. On the way, Jim handed the fatal weapon, his bone-handled six-gun, to the deputy.

The cross-examination of Crawford by the coroner and members of the jury was brief, but it added to the record the testimony that Sears' gun had not been fired and also that McKinney was, in Crawford's opinion, "boiling drunk." Crawford explained that McKinney had wanted to keep his gun until he arrived at the jail because he feared some of Sears' friends might attempt to avenge the death and he did not want to be unarmed.

Carey, who identified himself as a bartender at the nearby Reception Saloon, testified that he, McDonald, McKinney and Sears had gotten "roaring drunk" and there had been "a little wrangling," over what he could not say. The four left the saloon and went out into the alley. There, Carey said, Sears drew his gun and half playfully, half in earnest, punched the barrel toward McKinney's face several times and twirled the weapon around his finger by the trigger guard.

"I don't like that," Carey said he heard McKinney say several times to Sears in objection to the gunplay.

"We all started back to the saloon," Carey said. "Mc-
Kinney was about 10 or 12 feet in front. As the shot was
fired, I took McDonald by the arm and said, 'Let's go.'
"We went," he concluded.

Here one of the jurors interposed a question.

"Didn't you even turn around?" he asked.

"No sir!" said Carey emphatically. "I kept going."

"We went through the Palm Garden," he continued,
"and back to the Reception. I said to McDonald, 'let's
go eat,' so we went to the China restaurant and had
breakfast, but McDonald was sick and couldn't eat.
We went back to the alley and found Sears dead."

The coroner could not resist the temptation to ask
Carey if "your hair stood up a little" during the fracas,
and Carey gave him a straightforward answer.

"No sir. I had plenty of wine aboard and wasn't much
scared."

McDonald's testimony was even more vague than
was Carey's. He explained that his recollection of the
tragedy was obscured by the fog of alcohol. However,
the incidents he was able to recall corroborated the evidence given by Carey.

Meachem, the hack driver, emphatically told those
in the inquest room that he had seen the entire incident
from an excellent point of vantage and, unlike McDonald and Carey, was stone sober, having just arisen from
his bed with the refreshment of a good night's sleep.
It was his version of the shooting that was generally
accepted as the truth, but it was never to be presented
in a court of law. It was to be substantiated by McKinney himself two years later in a drunken boast that he

had gotten out of one murder and could get out of another.

"I was on the stairs of the Reception, coming from bed," Meachem said, indicating that he roomed above the saloon that adjoined the Cohn store.

"I had just gotten up. The stairs come down to the alley. Mac and Joe were pulling and hauling Sears and McKinney out there in the alley. Tom pulled his gun and made some kind of monkeyshines with it and they pulled them apart again.

"They were more than full, the whole bunch of them. McKinney pulled his gun out and there was a dog around their feet. Both pulled their guns and Mac and Joe got them apart again. McKinney started toward the Palm Gardens and Sears said to him, 'Let's shake hands, call it off, and be friends.'

"McKinney didn't want to shake hands at the start, but anyhow they came together and shook hands. They walked about twelve feet and some words passed. Joe and Mac were right behind Tom.

"Tom goes down like this (here Meachem slid from the witness chair to assume a kneeling position) and throws his gun about eight or ten feet away from him, over against Ramirez' wall, and says, 'Shoot, if you won't make friends!' "

At this point Meachem made a gesture indicating that Sears had thrown open his coat when he assumed the kneeling position.

"And quick as a flash McKinney done like that (here Meachem arose and pantomimed the act of a man

pointing his pistol down and firing at a kneeling man)
and the other man never struggled!"

Under cross-examination, Meachem showed how
Sears had opened his coat all the way in the sacrificial
gesture that was to be his last act on earth, and reiter-
ated that Sears "never suffered a bit." Meachem said he
saw Carey and McDonald hurrying away. He also saw
Crawford arrive on the scene, still hitching up his pants.

Sam DeBow, a bartender at the Last Chance Saloon,
which was located nearby, was next to take the stand.
Sam was in the OK Barber Shop nearby when he heard
the shot. The main point of his testimony was that he
went over to the alley and found Sears dying, but not
yet dead. He saw no pistol.

John Riley, who gave his occupation as porter for the
Ramiriz brothers, told how he was at the tearful task of
cleaning onions in the yard next to the alley when he
heard the quarrelling and peered through the gate. He
saw four or five men, including a tall one with a gun.
The dishwasher from Ramiriz' restaurant cautioned
him. "That's a bad 'un, look out!"

Riley prudently went back to his onions. When the
shot was fired, Riley returned to the gate, and seeing a
deputy sheriff on the scene, plucked up the courage to
go over and look at Sears.

"He was not yet dead. I touched his hand!" Riley
told the jury.

The porter commented that he saw a woman looking
out of a nearby window. He finished his testimony with
the statement that he saw Sears' pistol twelve or fourteen feet from the dying man's hand.

• 99

The next witness was a woman who was allowed to testify without, as had the other witnesses, first stating her occupation, a bit of chivalrous consideration on the part of the coroner. Her testimony was brief.

"I hear shot," she said in broken English, "but I no see."

When she had concluded, the coroner declared sufficient evidence had been heard to enable the jury to arrive at the cause of Sears' death. Reaching a verdict was easy and obvious. The six men were soon back with a formal statement to the effect that Thomas Sears had died from a gunshot wound inflicted by James McKinney. It was not the jury's duty to indict or exonerate, but merely to determine the cause of death. However, the district attorney took his cue from the testimony and the verdict. He ordered McKinney arrested and held to answer to a charge of first degree murder.

After Jim was jailed, he expressed to a reporter from the *Bakersfield Californian* who came to interview him in his cell a regret for the "necessity" of the shooting. He told the reporter that his friendship with Sears had dated back to the time both were kids in the east, and they had roomed together in Bakersfield.

"This much I can say," McKinney said in the interview, "I acted only in self defense. If I hadn't had to do it, it would not have happened.

"We were friends, but Sears was mean when he was drinking."

Assuming the truth of this last statement, then Jim McKinney had at least one characteristic in common with his victim.

100 ●

He added the information that he and Sears had been drinking together most of the night before the killing.

The *Californian* reported that when McKinney was jailed immediately after the shooting, he collapsed on his cot in a drunken stupor. When the jailer tried to rouse him, he muttered, "Let me alone, Tom. Let me sleep a little longer."

McKinney the ex-convict, gun-toter, gambler, and now killer, did not languish long in jail. His friends quickly rallied to his support with $5,000 bail fixed by the court. Among those who helped to raise the bail was Jeff Packard, who was to die at the hands of the outlaw just two years later.

Trial was held in Bakersfield May 10, 1901, and before the first witness was sworn it was conceded throughout the city that the prosecution had little chance for a conviction. Even had there been no evidence to show that McKinney acted in self defense, the feeling against the bully, Sears, ran so strong that among a substantial segment of the population there was a sentiment of gratitude to McKinney for ridding the city of a trouble-maker.

As the trial began, exhibits were filed with the clerk of the court, among them McKinney's weapon, a .44 Colt six-shooter. At last he had found a gun that would not miss fire.

McKinney's biggest break in the trial was the failure of the prosecution to produce Meachem, the hack driver, as a witness. Sometime between the inquest and the trial he left Bakersfield, and when the sheriff went in search of him to subpoena him for the trial, he was nowhere to be found. No one would say whether he had disappeared of his own volition or had vanished under force of bribery or threat. Another important prosecution witness who also vanished was Sam De-Bow, who had told the coroner's jury he had seen Red Sears' gun many feet from his body. John Riley, the onion peeler, was not even asked to testify.

One of Bakersfield's most able attorneys, J. W. P. Laird, who was one day to be on the opposite side of the courtroom in which McKinney's name was prominent, defended the killer. Laird was fortunate enough to find a witness who could explain in a manner favorable to the defense the reason for Sears' weapon being so far from his body. The witness, who said he was from Ventura County and his occupation that of farmer, explained that he had been visiting in Bakersfield. On the morning of the fatal shooting he had just visited the post office and was walking down the alley between 19th and 20th streets reading a letter when he heard a shot and looked up to see Sears falling mortally wounded. This Ventura farmer testified that as Sears fell, he threw his gun to one side, and the weapon landed several feet away.

Laird got in a good lick at Sears' reputation when he presented Dave Moshier, the proprietor of the Mint Saloon in Porterville and a friend of McKinney of long standing. Introducing himself to the jury, Dave gave his business as "sheep and whiskey." He testified that he had known the deceased in Porterville and that Sears had such a bad reputation he had been run out of that town.

This bit of testimony drew strenuous objection from the prosecution on the substantial grounds that Sears, having faced a sterner judgment, was not on trial. The judge sustained the objection, but the jury had heard the statement of Moshier. Laird had made his point that Sears was considered a no-good.

With the damning testimony of the hack driver, Meachem, lacking in court, and the plausible explanation given by the Ventura farmer regarding the distance the gun had been thrown from the body, plus a statement by Dr. Shafer that despite the smashing heart shot Sears might have lived long enough to throw his gun several feet away, the jury was out only a few minutes before bringing in a verdict:

"Justifiable homicide in self defense."

So far as the twelve jurors were concerned, there was no version of the shooting which involved Sears throwing his weapon away, opening his coat, and inviting his friend to shoot him. They had heard none of the witnesses make that statement. Someone obviously saw to it that no such witnesses were presented. The jury had no alternative but to acquit.

It may be assumed that there was considerable celebrating in the Bakersfield tenderloin that night.

VII

J AMES MCKINNEY, having finally made the grade as a full fledged killer, dropped out of the limelight of public print, but legend began to grow about him. His escapades, told and retold in the public bars, took on color and magnitude with the repetition. He was a well known and notorious character in every bar and gambling hall from Merced to Bakersfield, and he had only to step inside such a place to create a hush, a casting of furtive glances, and a speculation in the minds of those present as to the intentions of a man with such a reputation.

After the Sears episode, he extended his operations to the rough mining towns in the Mohave desert around Randsburg, where his brother, Ed, had opened a saloon. Bakersfield occasionally saw him, and he spent considerable time with Sarah in Porterville. She accompanied him on trips to the desert and spent a few weeks with him on the coast, around Santa Barbara and Ventura.

The exaggeration of his reputation as a badman is demonstrated by a story printed in one of the St. Louis papers during this period. The writer told of a poker game between McKinney and one of the Spanish California badmen. The game supposedly lasted throughout the night, and the Spanish desperado consistently held winning hands. However, said the St. Louis correspondent, he was so afraid of McKinney that he let the badman from Bakersfield bluff him purposely, and ended up broke.

Meanwhile, in Bakersfield Jeff Packard, one of McKinney's bondsmen in the Sears slaying, was appointed to the position of town marshal, filling the vacancy created by the death of George Tibbet. Jeff was a myopic, popular man, not impressive in stature but quick as lightning, sinewy, and as courageous as a wounded grizzly. Happy and smiling by nature, he loved excitement, even when accompanied by personal jeopardy.

"I never saw him taken in drink," recalled an old friend, "but he was friendly to a fault. I've seen him kick up his heels in a dance hall just for the sport of it."

He was a man's man who loved to ride, hunt and shoot. His trademarks were his thick lensed glasses and the stogie which was almost always clamped between his teeth.

106 •

"No braver or truer heart ever lived," the *Californian* was to say of him in eulogy two years after his appointment as marshal.

Although he was now branded as a killer, McKinney had not been an outlaw since paying his debt to society in state prison. He had nothing against his record from the time of his acquittal in the Sears slaying in Bakersfield until the hot night of July 27 when, in the town of Porterville, he killed again. Once more his victim was to be a close personal friend, and the killing was to be done without extenuating circumstances, but in a drunken rage during which he was to hold the town in terror for the greater part of a long and bloody night.

Porterville's prosperity had grown by the years, and as the town expanded it tried to shake off its pioneer ways and the traditional pioneer tolerance of vice.

Porterville had recently voted to incorporate as a city and one of the planks of the incorporation platform was that as a city, Porterville could have its own police system. Without the indirect control from the sheriff's office in Visalia, which was often uncertain and unreliable, it would be easier to outlaw the gamblers, guntoters, and whores.

The dream was easier than the reality. John Willis, the city marshal, a man well along in years, had tried out the city's authority by raiding some of the houses in the redlight district. His over-enthusiastic dragnet had swept up not only girls, but also a number of their customers, among them several brash young men scarcely out of their teens. The worldly men of the town, alert to pick out any flaw in the new government and loath to see the youthful wild-oat sowers brought to judgment, were quick to deride the efforts of the marshal. Willis found himself the subject of scornful comment as a pseudo-strict law enforcement officer who arrested mere boys while permitting such hardened characters as Jim McKinney to run at large and openly flaunt the law by not only patronizing, but also soliciting for a house of ill fame. The sports of the town claimed that there was one law for the gun-toting likes of Jim McKinney and his hard companions, and another for young men out for an innocent fling. Willis, in self-protection, was moved to turn the screws tighter on the gambling and prostitution element. He made no secret of the fact that he was out to get McKinney and all others of the same stamp who enriched themselves on the shortcomings of those who patronized the houses of vice.

The harassment of the vice element began to get on the nerves of McKinney, who was looked upon as the champion of the cause of those who favored the unrestricted operation of the establishments. He brooded over the clamp-down on his freedom and the threat to the profits to be made in the night life of the community. When a prominent man warned him to take it easy, as Willis was planning to answer the critics of law enforcement by raiding the very house where Sarah plied her profession and advised Jim to stay away from her a while, McKinney is said to have given an explosive reply.

"You go to hell," he is reported to have shouted at his well-intentioned advisor. "If any man ever kicks down a door on me, I'll shoot his head off."

The threatened raid, if planned, was delayed, but the pressure remained on Willis who, in turn, applied it to McKinney. Tempers on both sides became short and a showdown was merely a matter of time. It came in a sudden flare of excitement and tragedy that made Porterville certain it would never forget Jim McKinney.

The badman and his friend, Ralph Calderwood, sat drinking together in Dave Moshier's Mint Saloon on the night of July 27, 1902. Calderwood, better known to the town as Scotty, was the proprietor of the chop house which bore his name. The Mint was located in the heart of the two blocks of Main Street, almost centered in the business district, which contained most of the town's booze joints. Diagonally across, on the west side of the street was Scotty's Chop House, where Al Jones was tending bar and Art Kilbreth was cooking and serving short orders. It was a hot night, and in Scotty's an electric fan buzzed noisily on one end of the bar, its breezes cooling off late loungers who sipped beer or munched their snacks.

Across the street in the Mint, alcohol buzzed in the heads of McKinney and Calderwood, and they, too, became noisy. As Jim's surliness increased with each drink, the men in the place sensed his mood. Considering his sinister reputation, they had no desire to be around him when he was in such a condition. The games shut down as the players made excuses to leave. The barflies drifted to places where the atmosphere was less tense. Scotty, past realizing or caring what condition his drinking companion was in, remained with McKinney until the pair of them were the only ones in the place.

Across the street in the chop house, they could see much activity still going on, although the hour was late. In John Zalud's Saloon adjoining Scotty's on the south and connected to Scotty's by an arched entrance, the games were running full blast. McKinney and Scotty decided to move across the street to join in the fun.

At the chop house, McKinney blustered up to the bar, slapped down a $20 gold piece and ordered drinks for all hands. Kit Tatman, a good friend of both McKinney and Scotty, was among those who bellied up to have a drink.

The newcomers were roaring drunk. They argued and bragged over their prowess with guns. Kilbreth, with his back to the bar, while going about his business of cooking, heard Jim bet Scotty five dollars he could shoot a hole through the copper coffee urn that stood on the back bar without breaking any of the crockery on the shelves behind it.

"Of course I thought it was just drunken talk and he wouldn't do it," Art Kilbreth remembered fifty-four years later. "But he did!"

At sound of the shot, Art did just what characters in similar situations in western movies do. He hit the floor.

Kit Tatman's version of what happened bears up well for authenticity when compared with the less detailed account which appeared next day in the *Visalia Times*, probably the most reliable journalistic source of information on the affair since the destruction of the Porterville newspaper files by fire.

After shooting a precise hole through the coffee urn, McKinney looked for a more formidable target. His eye fell on the electric fan at the end of the bar. He leveled his gun at it and pulled the trigger. The bullet, Kit Tatman swore half a century later, hit the shaft of the fan dead center, stopping the blades immediately.

Calderwood hauled out his own gun to have a try, but in his alcoholic daze was unable to bring it to bear. McKinney grabbed the weapon away from him.

"Here, you Scotch son-of-a-bitch. I'll show you how," he boasted.

He waved Scotty's weapon around, seeking a likely target. Through the archway which opened into the Zalud Saloon next door McKinney saw a group of card players seated at a table sitting back to watch the fun. Flushed with the success of his marksmanship as well as with booze, Jim took aim at a stack of poker chips on the card table. He fired, and poker chips and players scattered in all directions.

When someone urged him to be careful, warning him that he might have killed one of the men at the table, the drink-crazed badman shouted that he had killed before and gotten away with it. This, said Tatman, was for the benefit of Marshal John Willis, who had just entered the place in response to a summons and was trying to placate McKinney with an appeal to reason.

"I can lick any two men who ever lived," McKinney roared. "The drunker I get the straighter I shoot."

He demonstrated by mowing down a row of vinegar cruets on the back bar. Willis promised him immunity from arrest if he would cease his shooting and go home. The marshal realized that he faced a dangerous situation. It was not so much for his own safety that he feared, as he was a brave man, as for that of others in the room.

"I was scared to death," Tatman said in recollection. "I thought everyone would be safer if Willis left, for his presence seemed to accentuate Jim's ugly mood. I talked Willis into leaving and when he went out the door McKinney calmed down a little, but he continued to fire his guns now and then.

"Drunk as he was, he was shrewd enough not to exhaust the ammunition in his own gun and Scotty's gun at the same time. One gun was always ready, and none of us had a chance to disarm him."

A little while later, Tatman edged out the front door onto the sidewalk. "About the time I came out, here came Willis back with his deputy, Johnny Howell, Deputy Constable Billy Tompkins, and a railroad man I remember only by the name of Lyons," Tatman said.

"As they came up, Jim and Scotty came out the door. I stepped to the edge of the board sidewalk to give them room. When Jim came out the door he turned to the right, and as he did so, he fell down. That's how drunk he was.

"It was then that they began shooting at him and he began shooting back."

The press version differed somewhat from that of Tatman. It stated that as McKinney met the peace officers on the sidewalk, he began shooting wildly.

"Jim, stop your shooting," Willis is reported to have called out to him.

Willis, when his command was not heeded, stepped back against the building and fired his snub-nosed revolver at McKinney. Intentionally or unintentionally, he failed to hit him at almost point-blank range. Tompkins fell, shot through the shoulder. Lyons was also wounded sufficiently to be retired from the fight.

His ammunition exhausted, McKinney turned and ran south, reloading as he ran. Willis, who carried a heavy cane, pursued closely and managed to clout the badman on the head, but the blow merely inspired the gunman to more speed. Willis fired his revolver, aiming low with the obvious intention of bringing down McKinney without inflicting a fatal wound. The bullet struck McKinney in the right leg, passing through the fleshy part about halfway between the knee and the hip.

McKinney had now succeeded in reloading. He turned and fired over his left shoulder. The bullet struck Willis just above the lip on one side of his nose, coming out through his mouth without making a serious wound but effectively discouraging the marshal from further pursuit, as he bled profusely.

There were those who were to say later that McKinney pistol-whipped the marshal, and that Willis acquired his wound in this manner, but Tatman's eyewitness statement is that Willis was wounded by a bullet from McKinney's gun which Tatman saw fired.

With three men out of the fight, the town's little police force was completely demoralized. With three men wounded, it was to offer no resistance to the outlaw during the two hours more he was to remain in town, shooting up the main business district and terrorizing those who were awakened by the noise. No one was able to rally a force of private citizens. There was never any organized resistance after Willis went down. McKinney was in charge.

"Men hid under the sidewalks and in the buildings," Tatman said of the terror that gripped the survivors. "They were afraid to do anything. I could have killed Jim McKinney a dozen times that night, but he was my friend, just like he was the friend of a lot of others who saw what happened."

But that didn't keep McKinney from trying to kill Tatman later that fatal morning.

It was about one-thirty when McKinney dropped Willis with a shot in the mouth. The badman, no longer pursued, crossed Main Street and doubled back to Oak Street, heading for the redlight district and Sarah's place, where he kept his shotgun and his rifle. It is also probable that he intended to see his mother, but he was not able to do so.

Meanwhile those around Scotty's recovered from their fright sufficiently to minister to the wounded and to summon a doctor. Billy Lynn and Clint Kelly, both young men about town like Kit Tatman, had witnessed the fracas in Scotty's and, realizing that McKinney was in for serious trouble, set out to find him. Clint said later that his intention was to plead with Jim to give himself up and, if he would not do that, to help him get out of town before he hurt someone else.

It happened that Lynn was about the same size and build as Marshal Willis and, like Willis, he wore a white hat that evening. McKinney's defenders blame this resemblance to Willis for the tragedy that was to occur, but others do not agree.

Lynn and Kelly started down the north side of Oak Street, heading east. As they crossed the intersection at the first block east of Main, they saw McKinney walking rapidly west on the south side of the street. He was carrying a rifle and a shotgun he had borrowed several days before to use on a ditch guarding job.

As Lynn and Kelly crossed the dusty street to intercept him, Jim blazed away at close range with the shotgun. Lynn went down in agonizing pain, his groin filled with a charge of birdshot. This is one version of the shooting of Lynn, the one told in the press. It assumes that McKinney thought Willis was coming to take him, and he was determined to kill Willis, his enemy, rather than be arrested.

There are others who say that McKinney realized full well the true identity of Lynn, and that they conversed, McKinney charging Lynn with wasting no time heading toward Sarah's house to pre-empt McKinney's claims on the girl just as soon as he figured McKinney was in trouble and would have to leave town. Clint, when he was able to talk about the incident, stuck with the mistaken identity version.

Whatever the truth is, Billy Lynn lay groaning in the street with wounds he would not survive despite two operations the following day, and McKinney was punching Kelly around with the barrel of his shotgun, threatening him with a dose of the same medicine he had just given Lynn.

"I am your friend, Clint Kelly," pleaded Clint, throwing his hands above his head. "You are not going to shoot me, too, are you?"

McKinney continued to curse Kelly, but decided to spare the trembling man. He turned and headed south toward the Arlington Stables, crossing the slough which bisects the business district of Porterville south of Oak Street. Kelly, speechless with fear, went back to Main Street, where he managed with some difficulty to give a coherent account of what had happened to Lynn.

Meanwhile the mortally wounded man had managed to drag himself to a nearby house, where he summoned the occupants with a rap on their door and begged for a drink of water. Lynn was to say bitterly before he died that those in the house were too frightened to venture out to aid him.

When Kelly was finally able to stammer out to Tatman and others at the chop house the fate of Lynn, his story struck new terror into the hearts of his listeners. Tatman tried to find someone who would go with him to help Lynn. The only volunteer was Old Man Wilcox. The two of them ventured cautiously down Oak Street and found Billy groaning on the sidewalk near the intersection of Oak and First Streets, still begging for a drink of water. They hastened back to a rooming house on Main Street and obtained a bedspring which they converted into a makeshift stretcher on which they moved Lynn to a bed in the Palace rooming house a block away.

Billy knew it was all off with him. He made the traditional gesture of the westerner dying of gunshot wounds. He asked Kit to remove his shoes, lest he die with them on.

Lest the modern reader become too hasty in condemning the citizens of Porterville for their seeming shortcomings in courage that night, harken back to the advice of Billy Carder on how to stay healthy in the frontier towns.

"Mind your own business."

In the rough society of Whiskey Row, self-sacrificial gestures were rare. A man who chose such associations was supposed to look out for himself. Most citizens were not abroad in the streets and saloons at such an hour and had no inclination to come out and risk their necks for those who were.

This reasoning applied to the reactions of Webb Loyd, one of the cooks at Scotty's who was not on duty that fatal night of July 27, 1902. Al Jones, the bartender, prudently leaving the scene of McKinney's rampage, ran two blocks to Loyd's house to tell him what was happening.

"Jim McKinney's on the loose and he's shooting up the coffee urn and all the dishes," Jones shouted at Loyd as soon as he had awakened him by pounding on his door.

"Get your clothes on and come on down," he begged.

Mrs. Loyd helped her husband to reach an easy decision. "You're not going out of this house tonight, Webb Loyd," she commanded.

In later years Webb Loyd was fond of recalling the incident, and related his reaction with a chuckle. "I told Al that my shift started at five o'clock in the morning, and when the time came, I would be there. When I finally went, it was on tiptoe all the way."

McKinney, after leaving Lynn and Kelly, made his way to the Arlington Stables two blocks to the south, where he aroused the two hostlers, Butler and King. He ordered them to hitch a team of horses to a buggy, instructing them at gun point to make haste and not take time even to dress.

As the two frightened men were preparing the team and rig, McKinney served notice on Porterville that his reign of terror was not over by stepping to the door of the livery stable and firing several shots from his rifle up Main Street toward the saloon row. If there were any who had summoned up courage to start a pursuit, they were effectively discouraged by the demonstration.

When the rig was ready, McKinney climbed up to the seat, made his guns ready at hand, and swung the team into Main Street, heading north. As he proceeded, he fired left and right with both shotgun and rifle, aiming at street lights, doorways, signs, any target.

As he neared the Oak Street intersection, he saw a man on the sidewalk. It was George Barron, an Irish type compositor for the *Enterprise* who had come down from his second floor room to see what all the shooting was about. Jim picked up his shotgun and as Barron, overcome with surprise as he saw the barrel of the weapon point toward him, started to run, McKinney let him have a charge of shot which struck Barron in

118 ●

the arm and the small of the back. Fortunately for Barron, McKinney was still using birdshot. Buckshot at such short range could have been fatal.

Nearby, on the east side of the street, a number of people had descended the stairway of another second floor rooming house. Like Barron, they had heard the gunfire and shouting and were curious to see what was going on. In the group was W. B. West, Kit Tatman's grandfather, a doughty pioneer who had seen many a fracas in his day. As Barron fell, wounded, McKinney aimed his shotgun at the group of which Old Man West was a member. There was a mad scramble to get up the stairs. West, lacking the agility of his more youthful companions, was last. The shotgun roared and West caught the full charge of birdshot in the seat of his anatomy.

Barron, interviewed next day by newspaper reporters, was grateful that his wounds were no worse. "God is good to the Irish," he commented, "or I'd be a dead man."

As for Old Man West, his wife picked birdshot out of his backside for weeks, a painful process which precluded any light-hearted comments on his deliverance.

After shooting Barron and West, McKinney proceeded north up Main Street, still firing his weapons, shooting up the town with reckless disregard for life and property. At the end of the Main Street business area, he turned east to the corner of Thurman and Second Streets, where his friend, employer, and protector, Dave Moshier, the man who had testified in his behalf in the Sears trial, lived. Jim was confident that he could trust Dave in any emergency.

McKinney jumped from his buggy and pounded on Dave's door. When Moshier opened up, he saw McKinney standing, wild-eyed, in the semi-darkness. "I've killed four or five men, and must leave," McKinney blurted out. "Give me all the cash you have."

McKinney handed Moshier the keys to the safe at the Mint Saloon, having been entrusted with them while on duty there before he started his late rampage.

"Tell the Indian to give you the $100 I have in the safe," he told Moshier, referring by nickname to Ed Isham, a bartender at the Mint, later a respected Porterville police officer.

"Tell Ed I've gone, that they'll never take me," he cried dramatically. "I'll die game. Tracy won't be in it with me. I'm going to the hills and I'll kill anyone who looks at me."

Dave, anxious to get rid of the drink-crazed man as soon as possible, quickly scraped up $62 in his house and handed the sum to his erstwhile employee. He was extremely relieved when McKinney whipped up his team and drove away into the darkness.

Dr. J. L. Hardeman lived on Putnam Street, east of Main Street. He had been summoned from his bed by an urgent message to come down town to help Dr. Barber attend several men wounded by gunfire. Hastily putting on his clothes, he had grabbed his medical kit and started on foot the few blocks from where he lived to Main Street and the Palace rooming house. He had gone only a block or two when he saw a buggy drawn by two horses dashing in his direction. Doc Hardeman had not been informed there was a drunken madman loose on the town, and thinking someone had come to pick him up, he stepped out into the street to hail the driver of the buggy.

As the driver pulled his team to a plunging halt, the physician found himself peering into the menacing barrel of a six-gun held by Jim McKinney.

"Get in here," McKinney commanded. "Where you going?"

Hardeman told him he was headed for town to treat a wounded man and asked if it were Jim who needed attention. The badman told him he had been wounded and needed treatment. The doctor felt the wound in Jim's right leg and ascertained that it was not serious. He speedily applied a bandage to it, lending industry to his skill under the occasional prodding of McKinney's gun.

"You're my friend, Doc," McKinney reassured him while still holding him under the threat of his gun.

Sensing the mania in his captor, Dr. Hardeman, who later said he believed himself to be as near to death as he had ever been in his life, wanted to get away as quickly as possible. He pleaded that he must go to treat the other seriously wounded men. When he did so, Jim confirmed the doctor's suspicions that McKinney was the one who had done the shooting.

"They've been trying to get me since this town was incorporated," he said bitterly. "Now I've gotten them."

The physician, who was graduated from St. Louis Medical College in 1887 before an Austrian physician had launched a new branch of medicine to be called psychiatry, resolved to try a new line. "How is your mother, Jim?" he asked.

The menacing mood of the outlaw slipped from him in an instant. He relaxed and lowered his gun and began to discuss with Dr. Hardeman the state of his mother's health as calmly as if he had been passing the time of day with him under normal circumstances. When the doctor promised to let Mrs. McKinney know that her son's wound was not serious, Jim bade the physician a respectful goodbye and permitted him to go on his way. Dr. Hardeman, true to the tradition of his profession, did not permit the experience to unnerve him. He operated on Billy Lynn with a steady hand early that morning and again later in the day. He also assisted Dr. Barber in treating the other wounded.

After leaving Dr. Hardeman, McKinney drove back to Oak Street where, either at his mother's house or at Sarah's, he picked up his little bob-tailed dog. He lingered for a time at Sarah's to bid her farewell before turning his rig north again.

Tatman, who had stuck close to the suffering Lynn and had helped to summon the physicians, was sent by Dr. Barber to arouse a druggist who roomed at the Pioneer Hotel. As Tatman reached the corner of the hotel building, he turned to see McKinney's rig pull into the Main Street intersection from the east, turning north as it did so. McKinney picked up his rifle and fired a single shot at Tatman.

"I thought I was running when I saw Jim, but when he pointed that gun at me and fired, I discovered I hadn't been running at all compared to the way I ran afterward," Tatman said.

The bullet struck the wall of the building just over Tatman's head, and a flying chip of brick knocked off by the shot struck Tatman on the arm as he scrambled for the safety of the doorway of the hotel.

"I thought my whole arm was gone," said Tatman, "but it only made a little blister."

McKinney drove northward out of town at a brisk pace. He could have taken his time. There was no one astir in Porterville that night who had the stomach to pursue him.

After many minutes had elapsed, men began to emerge from their places of refuge and gathered in an uneasy group in front of Scotty's Chop House to gain courage in gregarity and to discuss what must be done.

Old Doc Feemster, who had been called out into the country earlier to ease an expiring patient, was returning sleepily to town in his buggy. He was much surprised as he turned down Main Street to see a crowd of men turn startled faces toward him, then stampede like frightened sheep for the nearest cover, pushing and pulling, cursing and shouting in panic as they strove to be first through nearby doorways. When they found, to their relief, that it was not McKinney come back to kill them all, there was much timorous banter as they exchanged remarks on who had run the fastest.

As the faint light of the early summer dawn touched the tips of the towering Sierra peaks to the east, McKinney whipped his team northward, then east to follow the back roads in the first line of foothills. He knew he would soon be the quarry for the biggest manhunt the state had seen since Evans and Sontag had crossed up the posses ten years before. He knew also that safety lay in the protection of the hills and the hill folk who would give him shelter.

He was headed for the Dry Creek country near Lemon Cove, twenty miles east of Visalia where his cousin, Dee McKee, lived. He arrived there weary, hung over, with the wound in his leg beginning to throb, and soberly realizing the predicament he was in. McKee, after hearing as much as McKinney chose to tell, permitted the wounded man to rest a few hours at his house. Then he saddled a horse for McKinney, hung a bag of food on the saddle horn, and watched Jim ride on up the canyon toward higher country.

The next day, Sheriff Will Collins and a hastily organized posse took his trail early. Near the bridge across the Kaweah River north of Lemon Cove they found the rig and team from the Arlington Livery Stable, with McKinney's little dog faithfully on guard. They traced McKinney to McKee's house, and he told them that the outlaw had fled hours ahead of them.

Thus started one of California's biggest manhunts. It was to last the better part of the year, would lead over much of the inhospitable California and Arizona desert country and even deep into Old Mexico before it would finally end in a bloody war to the death in the Chinese joss house in Bakersfield's tenderloin.

The newspapers had little faith in the ability of the peace officers to bring the murderer of Billy Lynn to a quick accounting. "Here is a foxy fellow, well armed,

124 •

and a dead shot," commented an editor, putting the odds in McKinney's favor.

Ben Maddox, the editor of the *Visalia Times*, made good the opportunity to gibe at the rival community of Porterville over the disgraceful episode, although Visalia, scarcely ten years before, had tolerated an almost equally errant son, Chris Evans, protecting him from justice.

Maddox righteously admonished his readers that a town in which so many men were abroad in such company at such late hours on Sunday night, in which so many led such maudlin lives, could not expect to have the virtue of valor. He accused the decent citizens of Porterville with being derelict in their duty in permitting wide-open boozing, gambling, and worse.

"Good men may close their eyes," wrote Ben Maddox, who once had lost his pile at the gambling tables of old Bodie at a youthful age when experience costs dearly, "but they do not deceive themselves when they acquiesce in the granting of licenses to conduct dives wherein fallen women congregate and disreputable gamblers find their prey."

• •   •
   •   •

VIII

$\mathcal{S}$ HERIFF COLLINS was well aware that he was dealing with a desperate and dangerous man. McKinney had boasted he was out to improve on the record of Bloody Harry Tracy, who at that time was on a 60-day spree of murder in the Pacific Northwest which would set him down in the annals of Oregon as that state's most vicious killer.

Tracy had spent much of his youth in prisons and was described by a prison warden who had been his host as having "many strong points to qualify him for a successful criminal career—nerves of steel, lightning decision and a reckless dare-devil attitude." Tracy had killed his first man before he was twenty.

On June 9, 1902, at the hardened age of 25, Tracy and a prison pal, Dave Merrill, engineered a sensational break from the Oregon State Prison at Salem and inaugurated the Northwest's bloodiest reign of terror since Indian days. Before he had finished, Tracy had killed seven men, wounded two others, and had taken several terrified persons as hostages before he was finally trapped in a swamp near Creston, Washington, by four men and a boy who killed him on August 5, 1902, and collected the $1,500 reward.

Tracy's lack of chivalry is illustrated by an incident of the chase. He and Merrill, who had been boyhood chums, had a falling out during the flight and arranged a duel with pistols. They were to stand back to back, each walk ten paces, turn and fire. Tracy is reported to have taken no more than sufficient steps to permit him room to whirl and shoot. Merrill dropped with a bullet in his back as he conscientiously carried out his part of the agreement, the victim of misplaced trust.

Tracy could never have commanded the loyalty of friends that was given McKinney. Tracy was bloodthirsty even when sober, as McKinney was not. Despite the brutal shootings in Porterville, a considerable amount of sympathy for McKinney still existed. The reform movement in Porterville was not uniformly popular. Even some respectable men thought it premature and ill-advised. Many believed McKinney had been goaded unjustifiably; the cold blood killing of Lynn was excused as a case of mistaken identity, although this carried the inference that the killing of

Willis, who represented law and order, would have been proper.

"No one, not even Doc Hardeman, would have turned Jim in," is the way Kit Tatman explained away the reluctance of Porterville citizens to try to take the outlaw into custody.

What is rumor and what is truth concerning McKinney's movements after he left Dee McKee's place is difficult to determine. It is fairly well established that he spent the second night of his flight at the Horse Creek ranch of Hale Tharp, a rugged old pioneer who achieved a place in history by discovering the big redwoods in the upper tributaries of the Kaweah River in the place now known as Giant Forest of Sequoia National Park. Hale's step-grandson, Will Swanson, was to remember the visit almost too well for his own good.

During the next few days, McKinney doubled back to the south, working his way along the foothills until he reached a point east of Porterville. Here he camped in hideouts until he could make contact with his brothers and friends to determine how best to conduct himself as a fugitive.

It is said he chose for his base of operations a granitic mountain known as Porterville Rocky Hill, a rugged landmark near McKinney's home community. To this day, a spring on the hill is known to old-timers as McKinney's Spring, as he is supposed to have lived in a sheepherder's or homesteader's shack nearby.

He was well supplied with two necessities, food and information on the movements of Sheriff Collins' men. Both were supplied through the cooperative efforts of

Jim's friends, his brothers, and of course his paramour, Sarah, whom he is said to have visited almost nightly during the several days he remained near Porterville.

Late one evening, when it was almost dark, Chester Doyle was coming into Porterville with a team and wagon heavily laden with lumber from the mountains. As he drove through the settlement at the east edge of Porterville, known as Doyle's Colony, a figure stepped from the darkness and grasped the bridles of his leaders, stopping his six-horse team. Doyle was not surprised to recognize Jim McKinney as the man who had stopped him. He handed Doyle a note. It was a request to be delivered to Dave Moshier, asking for money.

As Doyle was on friendly terms with McKinney and regarded him with considerable awe, he agreed to do the outlaw's bidding and made arrangements with McKinney for a rendezvous later in Success Valley, a few miles to the east.

When Doyle reached town, he delivered McKinney's note to Dave Moshier at the Mint Saloon. Moshier said not a word, but opened his safe and took $200 in gold from it, handed it to Doyle, and instructed him to deliver it to the outlaw. Doyle completed his mission.

With the money from Moshier to aid him, McKinney struck east over the mountains and headed for a remote ranch near Kingman, Arizona, where he might safely hide until the Porterville affair blew over.

On the way he stopped for three days at White River, where he hid in the barn of the Mitchell brothers, well known residents of the area who kept a well known hotel. On the third day, Mike Mitchell brought him to the house where Auntie Mitchell, the mother of the Mitchell brothers, and petite, pretty Debe Mitchell, Mike's wife, fed him buttermilk, cookies, and other delicacies for which the hotel was famous. Jim discussed the state of his mother's health with the two women and told Debe that at times he could have reached from his hiding place in the barn and touched her as she went about the daily chore of gathering eggs. McKinney was still suffering from the wound in his leg and was barely able to get around.

From White River McKinney rode over the next line of mountains to the comparative safety of Linn's Valley. Folks there had learned, from the realities of isolation, a tolerance that precluded the borrowing of trouble. Fugitives from the law were common in their part of the mountains, and as long as the outlaws minded their own business no one bothered them.

McKinney crossed the Linn Valley road near the Hughes ranch and encountered Mrs. Hughes working in her yard. He stopped to inquire the way to Jim Dunlap's cabin. Mrs. Hughes told him he could take either the wagon road or a trail. He chose the less traveled trail.

McKinney remained with Dunlap as an unwelcome guest for several days, until the wound in his leg had healed sufficiently to permit him to travel on toward the desert. In the course of his visit, word spread to the residents of Linn Valley of McKinney's presence among them. Dunlap, fearing trouble, asked McKinney to be on his way. McKinney induced two young men, Henry Connor and Bill Payton, to act as his guides over Green-

• 131

horn Pass to the east, and he selected a dark night on which to make the trip.

Connor was to relate in future years a brief encounter with McKinney's desperate nature which impressed him and Payton that their job had a sinister side. In the darkness, Connor and Payton temporarily lost the trail.

"Jim poked us with the barrel of his shotgun and allowed that by God we'd better find it quick if we knew what was good for us. You never saw two fellers look as hard for anything in the dark as me and Bill did for that trail, and we sure were glad when we found it," Connor said.

McKinney left them in the open country at the summit of the pass and disappeared into the desert to the south.

Sheriff Collins may not have been a spectacular law enforcement officer, but he was persistent. He bided his time, waiting for the fragments of information to trickle in to him from the saloon society in sufficient quantity to form a pattern. He learned that McKinney had been seen in Randsburg and elsewhere in the Mohave mining country on the California side, and that Sarah had made a trip over to visit him. As the weeks passed, Collins' informers passed along the information that Jim had moved his base of operations to Arizona and had been seen in the company of Jack Jeffords, a former Visalian who was a fugitive from a charge of cattle rustling. Law enforcement officers in Arizona began to suspect the pair of being responsible for new outbreaks of crime in the territory.

132 •

In the fall of the year, Bill Swanson's mother and stepfather went to Kingman, in Mohave County, Arizona. Kingman was at the time a busy mining center, a thriving frontier town located at the summit of a picturesque mountain pass of historic significance.

Will made a trip over to Kingman to visit his parents and while there had a chance encounter with McKinney that was to leave him shaken. Swanson was standing on a street corner one day talking with an acquaintance when a bearded man walked by. Swanson turned to watch the passerby. "I know that man," Swanson told his companion, "but I can't place him."

He followed the bearded individual down the street, and when he turned into a saloon, Swanson, too, pushed through the swinging doors. Inside, he saw the bearded man standing with his back to the bar, facing the entrance. Swanson had the opportunity to look the man whom he had been following squarely in the face, and suddenly realized with a shock that the bearded man was the notorious outlaw, Jim McKinney, who had spent a night at the home of Swanson's stepfather shortly after the Porterville shooting.

As the implications of recognition began to dawn on him, Swanson stopped. McKinney had a price on his head and had been publicized throughout the nation as a candidate for the title of the West's worst badman. A person not in his full confidence who knew of his whereabouts could be in grave personal danger.

Swanson made no sign of recognition and made as nonchalant an exit as he could. He hurried back to his friend on the street corner. "I've just seen Jim McKinney and I think he knows I recognized him," he told his friend. "I think it would be wise for me to get out of town."

Swearing his friend to secrecy, Swanson mentioned the incident to no one else and shortly thereafter returned to California. He was to carry with him the rest of his life the mental image of McKinney standing at the bar in the Kingman saloon, his coat thrown back and his hand near his six-gun, waiting for Swanson to make the wrong move or say the wrong thing.

In November of 1902, the *Visalia Times* printed an editorial commending the continuing efforts of Sheriff Collins in trying to run to earth an outlaw who was obviously shielded by so many influential friends. Other than the editorial comment little journalistic note was taken of McKinney in the California papers. However, he was the subject of half-true, half-fictional feature stories for midwestern and eastern papers which sought to liven up their pages with western blood-and-thunder. Typical of these was a cartoon-illustrated yarn in one of the St. Louis papers relating an encounter McKinney was supposed to have had with a notorious badman, a descendant of the Spanish Californios and heir to the reputation of the non-existent Murietta and the very real Tiburcio Vasquez—the previously mentioned incident where McKinney and the Spaniard had engaged in a poker game, where the Spaniard, through fear, had permitted McKinney to bluff him out.

Meanwhile, Sheriff Collins persisted in his efforts to bag such a prominent criminal, enlisting the aid of Arizona peace officers in attempting to follow his movements. They turned the heat on McKinney to such a degree that McKinney and his new side-kick, Jeffords, decided to go to Mexico until things cooled down a bit. Collins received a tip-off that Jim was below the border and undoubtedly would have gotten his bracelets on the fugitive had he been able to obtain the cooperation of Mexican authorities. It was the period when Mexico was a haven for a good many lawbreakers from the Southwest, and their influence often gave them the protection of petty Mexican officials.

After fixing McKinney's hide-out as being in a small town well below the border, Collins telegraphed Governor Pardee of California to start extradition proceedings. Collins and a deputy, Johnny White, left at once for Mexico, there to put the fugitives under surveillance until they heard from the governor.

Collins and White cooled their heels in Hermosillo and Prieta for three weeks while their expenses mounted, waiting for the exceedingly slow mill of Mexican statemanship to grind out the necessary papers. In desperation Collins wired Pardee. "My man here. Can do nothing until the governor gets instructions from the secretary of state."

Collins and his deputy went each day to the police station to see if the papers had come. They frequently saw McKinney and Jeffords in the taverns and observed that Jim was now smooth-shaven and had darkened his skin to more nearly resemble the Mexicans.

It may be assumed that the outlaws were kept well informed concerning the progress of the extradition proceedings, for just before the proper papers arrived which gave Collins permission to arrest the pair, they pulled out for parts unknown, leaving Collins empty-handed and disgusted. He returned to Visalia.

However disappointed Collins might have been, he continued his search so relentlessly that McKinney, in desperation for the money any fugitive finds imperative to have and hard to get legitimately, was goaded into committing a crime so horrible that it recalled his hysterical boast to Dave Moshier. "Tracy won't be in it with me!"

On April 6, Sheriff Collins received a telegram from Sheriff Henry Lovin of Mohave County, Territory of Arizona, that McKinney had killed two men near Cedar Creek, south of Kingman, and was being pursued toward California by a posse.

"Those double murders in Arizona were Jim's big mistake," in the opinion of his friend Kit Tatman. "The Arizona sheriff put an Indian trailer on him and ran him across the desert with no chance to rest."

Here is the story of McKinney's most cold blooded crime as told in the April 11, 1903, issue of the *Mohave Miner*:

"Last Wednesday morning Charles Blakey and Roy Winchester were murdered near the summit of the Wallapai mountains on the old Trecher road to Cedar. Their bodies lay where they had fallen from their horses until discovered by Sheriff Lovin late Saturday evening.

"Blakey and Winchester contemplated opening a saloon at the S. F. mining camp near Cedar and arranged to lease a building from A. O. Eshom. They went to Eshom's ranch near Copper Camp, where they stayed

136 •

Tuesday night. Eshom stated that he had received a letter stating that a brother of a miner at Cedar was very ill, and left the house early in the evening to deliver the message, agreeing to meet the men at Cedar the following day and deliver possession of the building.

"He remained at Cedar until Thursday noon, but the two men did not turn up and he came back to his house where he found McKinney, who informed him that he had had trouble with two men back on the road. McKinney then ordered Eshom to shoe a couple of horses, and packing them with provisions, he rode away, warning Eshom not to inform the sheriff until three days had passed.

"The sheriff went down the next morning and at dusk came upon the horses ridden by Blakey and Winchester. A short distance on, he found the bodies of the murdered men in the road. They had been shot with buckshot. The coroner was notified and the sheriff came to Kingman to organize a posse and go in pursuit of the fiend. The posse is made up of Lovin and Deputies Templeman, Harris, Bly, Wells and Piema, a Wallapai Indian trailer. They got on the trail Sunday evening.

"When Blakey and Winchester left Kingman, they were supposed to be possessed of nearly $500, but only $1.60 was found on their bodies.

"An inquest was held at Cedar but the jury failed to fix the responsibility for the killings. It appeared from the testimony that Dig Eshom arrived at the S. F. mine about two o'clock and called out Jim McKinney, who had been working at the mine under the name of Mc-

• 137

Intyre. McKinney at once bundled up his effects and left the camp without drawing the money due him for his work or saying why or where he was going. This, taken with the statement of Eshom that McKinney had had trouble on the road was convincing that this man had done the killings.

"The jury found that the man had ambushed the two and had fired without a word of warning. The murderer had fired the first shot from behind a small, scrubby tree. The first shot had evidently killed Blakey and had frightened Winchester's horse. The assassin then rose up and fired the other barrel, the charge taking effect in the boy's back.

"Death in both cases must have been instantaneous. Blakey had evidently thrown up his hand when the first shot was fired and part of the charge passed through it. He was struck in the breast and throat, and one shot passed into the head at the corner of the eye. Winchester was struck in the back by 13 shot and a hand would cover the wound. The bodies were taken to Undertaker Emerson and burial Wednesday was a most impressive affair.

"McKinney was followed to the Colorado River and on into California by Lovin. McKinney was heard of at Manvel and the horses of the posse were loaded on cars and a special train was taken to Ivanpah at the end of the California Eastern track. The gain on the fugitive was about 80 miles and left the posse about 36 hours behind.

"McKinney has a reputation as a killer, having killed two in California. He came to Mohave County about

138 •

eight months ago to escape the law and had been at the Dig Eshom ranch. When he arrived he was accompanied by a woman but she went back to California about six weeks ago. He is described as an all-around badman who knows no law but force.

"Blakey was a warm-hearted, generous man, a resident of the Territory for about 20 years. He came from Maine and leaves a wife and two children. Winchester was a young miner and came from Yuma. He had a host of friends. Eshom was jailed but was released on $1,000 bail."

Arizona was used to cold-blooded killings, but the magnitude of the slaying of Charles Blakey and Roy Winchester was such that it was to live in the history of Mohave County as a prime example of the violence of the formative years. Ace Harris, undersheriff of the county at the time, was to recall more than half a century later that as a badman Jim McKinney had the respect of the traditionally courageous lawmen of Arizona. "He had a cold heart, steady nerves, and the ability to shoot straight and ride hard," is the way Harris summed up the essential characteristics of the proper outlaw.

Harris was not in the posse which took McKinney's trail, but he was well aware that the brave men who did so knew full well the peril of the pursuit.

The *Mohave Miner's* story is not complete in detail. It leaves many questions concerning the crime unanswered, and fifty years later it was possible to obtain two different versions from those who could remember the tragedy. One version left a blight on the name of

● 139

Dick, for despite the *Miner's* reference to him as Dig, he seems to have had a more conventional name, Eshom. To be reasonably charitable, one must in the light of history give Eshom the benefit of the doubt. He seems to have been the unwilling victim of circumstances. There is little question that he knew he was harboring a desperate outlaw, but there is also little question that he was not quilty, as many thought him to be, of putting Jim up to the killing of Blakey and Winchester. The fact that he went to Kingman to tell Sheriff Lovin of "the trouble" at Cedar absolves him of blame. Had he been guilty, he would have kept his mouth shut and gone about his business, leaving the gruesome discovery of the bodies to time and chance.

There are those who believe that Dick Eshom knew Jim McKinney in Tulare County, but this is highly doubtful. Eshom was born in Tulare County, in the little mountain valley named for his pioneer father, but it is probable that the Eshom family left the county long before McKinney arrived in California from Leadville. The fact that McKinney had a friend in Porterville named Ed Isham, no relation to Dick Eshom, may have led Arizonans to confuse the names. An old county map in the road superintendent's office in Kingman today carries the location of Eshom's ranch near Cedar as "Isham's Ranch."

Ace Harris was with Sheriff Lovin when Dick Eshom came to Kingman to report the crime. Harris and Lovin were conversing on the street when Eshom approached them and told them there had been some kind of "trouble" at Cedar and suggested that Lovin go down there

140 ●

and investigate it. Lovin replied that the superintendent of the San Francisco mine was a deputy sheriff and if there had been any trouble he would have informed Lovin.

Eshom went on his way, and Lovin and Harris talked over his strange request; the sheriff asked his undersheriff for his advice. "I told him I would throw Eshom in jail and go down to find out what was bothering him," Harris recalled.

A few minutes later, Eshom returned and renewed his plea to the sheriff. Again he refused to be specific regarding the nature of the trouble but implied it was of a sufficiently serious nature to merit the personal attention of the sheriff.

Lovin took Harris' advice. He clapped Eshom in jail and early next morning set off for Cedar. He reached there near dusk and his findings were much as set forth in the newspaper article except that the horses were found at Eshom's ranch, and the saddle was gone from Blakey's horse, McKinney having taken it.

With Eshom in jail, Sheriff Lovin's next move after hurrying back to Kingman was to organize a pursuit of the killer. It is probable that Eshom revealed the identity of McKinney as the perpetrator of the deed only after the sheriff returned as, according to Eshom's statement, he had been warned by McKinney to allow plenty of time for Jim to make a get-away. After sending the coroner to take care of the bodies, Lovin chose Jefferson Davis Templeton, John Harris, no relation to Ace, Charles Wells, and a man named Bly to accompany him on the chase across the desert. The posse en-

listed the aid of Piema, a Wallapai Indian whose ability
to trail men or animals in the desert bordered on the
supernatural.

"No braver band of men ever went after a criminal in
this territory," declared the editor of the *Mohave Miner*.

Another story has persisted throughout the years
that Blakey and Winchester were not on a saloon purchasing mission at all, but had learned that McKinney
was at Cedar and deliberately set out to capture him
to earn the reward on his head. Lon Gibney, an old-
timer in Bakersfield, told his friends in after years that
he had encountered Blakey and Winchester on the
streets in Kingman, armed to the teeth, and they said
they were going after the outlaw. The State of California had placed a reward of $1,000 for his capture. After
Blakey and Winchester were slain, Mohave County offered $500 and the governor of the territory an addi-
tional $500. If Blakey and Winchester hoped to collect
the reward, it is ironical that in failure they merely
succeeded in making the prize twice as rich for the
ultimate winner. As it turned out, those who were eventually to collect were to pay a high price indeed.

The complete story of the circumstances which set
up the Arizona slayings will probably never be known,
for the inquest records are lost and the newspaper accounts are sketchy. It is not probable that Blakey, who
knew the desperate character of McKinney, would
have started out to capture him with the assistance of
so untried a companion as Winchester, who was little
more than an adolescent. Ace Harris did not believe

142 •

that the two victims of McKinney's shotgun had deliberately embarked on a manhunt.

It also seems unlikely that Eshom would set McKinney on two men who were coming to make a business deal with him for the lease of the saloon at the San Francisco mine, even for a split of the loot. Eshom was to testify before the grand jury that the outlaw had come down off the mountain road leading the horses of Blakey and Winchester. McKinney sat calmly at Eshom's kitchen table and carefully cleaned the fancy French-made shotgun which had just snuffed out two lives. He ordered Eshom to prepare him a pack of food and saddle up a pair of the fine horses that Eshom kept at his ranch, and to put Blakey's saddle which was a good one, on the better riding horse of the pair. Eshom's story to the grand jury was only that McKinney had told him he had had trouble with two men on the mountain, hinting that he had killed them both. He warned Eshom on pain of the same fate not to notify the sheriff until McKinney had a three-day start.

McKinney actually was to have a four-day start on Lovin's posse. Late March and early April had been marked by snow flurries and showers in the desert, a fact which made it possible for him to cross the normally dry area without having to stop at the mines and villages for water. The same advantage favored the posse, and it averaged more than fifty miles a day for the first two days, which can be considered excellent time under conditions as they existed. Piema had no difficulty following the tracks of the two freshly shod horses McKinney was using. The trail led straight west

• 143

from Cedar across the mountains, striking the Colorado
River about six miles upstream from old Fort Mojave,
the headquarters of the Indian reservation. McKinney,
the posse learned, had avoided using the ferry and had
hired an Indian to row him across in a boat, the horses
swimming behind.

Sheriff Lovin and one of the deputies, Harris, stuck
with the pursuit for another day across the river into
California, when the trail began to become more difficult, slowing the posse's progress. It became evident
that no quick contact with the outlaw would be made.
Lovin received reliable information that McKinney
had been seen at Ivanpah which was the terminus of
the California Eastern Railroad. He turned the command of the posse over to Templeman and put it on the
train for the 80-mile trip to Ivanpah, instructing Templeman to take up the trail from there, while Lovin and
Harris returned to Kingman to take up Eshom's case
before the grand jury.

McKinney, after crossing the Colorado, proceeded
north, stopping at isolated mines and cattle camps to
which news of the Arizona murders had not yet pene-
trated. Although the posse gained a day and a half on
him by taking the train, the advantage amounted to
little. The trail led on through the inhospitable desert
to Saratoga Springs at the southern end of Death Valley.
Templeman was always faced with the disturbing fact
that should his little band of men close up with McKinney, the outlaw might ambush them in some narrow,
rocky canyon and shoot them down in cold blood just
as he had Blakey and Winchester. The advantage was

with the fugitive, who was well armed and a dead shot. But Templeman went resolutely on. He and his men rested briefly at Randsburg and were only forty miles from Bakersfield on April 19 when Jim McKinney was finally run to earth.

Melvill Templeman was only six years old when his father accepted the hazardous job of posseman, but he retained a lifetime remembrance of the evenings at home during his father's absence. Each evening his mother spent an interlude in tears and prayer as her thoughts turned to her husband and the chance of what might occur should he encounter the dreaded outlaw in the desert. Neighbors were more than usually kind to a little boy who might soon be a half-orphan, Melvill recalled.

Mrs. Templeman and the neighbors need not have worried. McKinney's grey and bay horses withstood the challenge of the desert and conveyed the outlaw to the comparative safety of the High Sierra before he abandoned them to finish his journey on foot.

When Sheriff Lovin returned to Kingman, the grand jury assembled to probe into the innocence or guilt of Dick Eshom as an accomplice in the evil deed on the mountain. Eshom's explanation of his relationship with McKinney was straightforward. The outlaw had come to his ranch several months before, posing as a roving cowboy in search of work. Good hands were hard to find on Arizona ranches and it was a code of the times not to question prospective employees too closely concerning their past. McKinney was using the name of his friend in Porterville, Tom McIntyre, and Eshom had no reason at the time to doubt his word.

Eventually Eshom was to discover the true identity of his hired hand, who left frequently and was gone for long periods. After his sojourn in Mexico, McKinney returned again to the ranch and went to work in the mine, although he continued to stay at the Eshom ranch. The rancher was frank to tell the jury that he had harbored a fugitive, but did so because of fear of what might happen to him if he informed.

Eshom's brother-in-law, John Sweeny, an attorney, led him safely past the shoals in his testimony. If much remained unclear to the general public, it was at least clear to the grand jury that Eshom did not have a part in the killings and did not profit from them.

What did McKinney's loyal friends think of him now? Those who had aided him in evading the law might well bow their heads in shame and assume a measure of responsibility for the deaths of warm-hearted, generous Blakey and Winchester, the miner from Yuma who was just a kid. Instead, the reaction of most of them, as well as of his two brothers, Ed and Jake, was to refuse to believe the obvious truth. They believed with stubborn persistence that Jim could not be capable of committing so cold-blooded a crime. They continued to assist him.

The deaths of Blakey and Winchester set the law on McKinney in grim earnest. In the two weeks from the time he killed them until he wound up on a slab in Bakersfield, the chase was played up on every front page in the West. The San Francisco newspapers, sensing a spectacular western style gun battle was in the making and a story that would rival the Evans and Sontag saga of the previous decade, sent their top reporters to Kern County to be in at the kill.

In addition to the Arizona posse, two others were soon to take McKinney's trail. Sheriff James Kelly of Bakersfield assembled an able and fearless group of men, among them Dan Overall, McKinney's old Nemesis. Overall was no longer sheriff of Tulare County, having taken up business pursuits in which he was highly successful, but through the grapevine had come reports that McKinney had vowed vengeance on Overall and boasted he would shoot him on sight. Dan Overall was a proud and fearless individual who would not tolerate such a challenge to go unheeded. He was eager to extend the feud between himself and McKinney to any degree the outlaw chose. He always considered it unfortunate that his business affairs required him to be in Visalia the weekend McKinney was trapped in Bakersfield. Overall wanted to be in at the kill, and McKinney was to mistakenly believe in his last moments on earth that he was.

Sheriff Collins of Tulare County, whose relentless pursuit of the outlaw had been one of the factors which finally forced McKinney's hand, brought his own posse into the picture, working closely with Lovin and Kelly. At Needles, on the California border, Undersheriff Walter Brown of San Bernardino County got into the chase. On April 8, he wired Kelly that McKinney had crossed the river and was headed for his old haunts in Kern County.

• 147

As might have been suspected, McKinney was to be reported in a dozen localities at the same time. During the ten days preceding his death he was seen in so many places that the sheriffs began to think that there was a deliberate plot to throw them off the trail. Descriptions of his appearance were as varied as the reports of his whereabouts. He was seen bearded, smooth-shaven, with handlebar moustaches, with his hair dyed, drunk, sober, tired and hungry, vigorous and well fed, on horseback and afoot. The newspapers were so eager for news of him that they printed the wildest of rumors as well as poorly substantiated facts.

McKinney was not enjoying the role of fugitive. On his flight through the inhospitable desert he had to keep to the back roads and rugged desert trails. The eager Lovin-Templeman posse with its Indian tracker gave him no opportunity to rest. His brother, Ed, and his friends in the Randsburg area were so closely watched he could not expect to find a haven there. Jim left Porterville a strong, virile man whose stocky frame was well filled out, according to Art Kilbreth, who saw him on the night of the fracas at Scotty's Chop House. Art was to see him in Bakersfield the night before his death and was shocked at McKinney's emaciated appearance. He was so thin and worn Kilbreth scarcely recognized him.

On April 9, the *Bakersfield Californian* reported that Sheriff Ralphs of San Bernardino County had joined the pursuit, and that McKinney had been seen at Manvel, about two days' ride from Randsburg, toward which everyone assumed McKinney would head. A newspaper carried a story that Jake McKinney was missing from his customary haunts around Porterville and was assumed to be on his way to Radamacher, twelve miles from Randsburg, where Ed McKinney was operating a saloon.

"That McKinney is possessed of an unholy desire to imitate the career of Tracy is becoming more apparent every day," said the *Californian.* "The officers are determined to do their best to thwart that desire. The outlaw now has four murders and three shootings to his credit, besides other offenses known. There is a strong suspicion that he knows something of other crimes in Arizona where holdups and robberies followed his return from Mexico."

Ed and Jake McKinney, realizing the sinister quality of the pursuit and suspecting that their brother would be given little chance for his life if caught by men who both feared and hated him, began frantically to work out a truce with Sheriff Lovin, whom they considered the most unlikely to take him alive. However, Ed and Jake were so closely watched they had little opportunity to make contact with Jim.

Randsburg filled up with men on the lookout for the outlaw—newspaper reporters, peace officers, and "gentlemen from San Francisco and Stockton who refuse to discuss their business with the outlaw" but who were probably journalists in search of exclusive stories such as Joaquin Miller had obtained from Chris Evans at his mountain hideout many years before. Despite the vigil, McKinney was reported to have passed through Randsburg on April 8, although it is extremely doubtful that he actually did so.

"There is no doubt," said the *Bakersfield Echo* with misguided confidence, "in the mind of Sheriff Kelly that McKinney is now hiding in the Radamacher district where the murderer's two brothers, Ed and Jake, reside, and it is believed that they will aid their brother to the last ditch. It will be a hazardous undertaking to locate the outlaw. He is thoroughly familiar with the country and the topography favors his efforts to resist arrest. The country is mountainous and the hills are honeycombed with mine tunnels and shafts."

The *Echo's* guess was a poor one. McKinney was a gregarious individual who preferred to take his chances hiding among his friends in the towns than in the lonely hills of the desert.

The grand jury had scarcely completed its investigation of Eshom in Kingman than Sheriff Kelly telegraphed Sheriff Lovin, asking him to join the Kern County posse, as McKinney was expected to make his appearance soon in Kern County. Lovin grumbled that he had expended a large amount of his own money on the chase already, and his share of the reward, assuming that he helped to capture the outlaw, would scarcely compensate him for his trouble.

McKinney tarried but very little in the Randsburg country, if he went through it at all, but hastened as fast as his weary horses would carry him up to Inyo Valley, entering Kern County by crossing the Sierra from the east by way of Walker Pass. In the mountainous east side of Kern County he had many friends in the ranching and mining settlements who would hide him and feed him as he passed their way. As the peace officers suspected he might head that way, the country was well patrolled.

On April 12, two of Kelly's deputies, McCracken and Warren Rankin, were riding in the mountains northeast of Bakersfield at Canebrake Spring on the historic Walker Pass trail when they saw a lone horseman on the road. They reined their horses toward him to make a routine check of his identity. As they did so, the rider drew a rifle from his saddle scabbard and fired at the deputies. They dismounted and returned the fire as the man wheeled his horse and rode off into the brush and trees. The deputies remounted and pursued, but found the man was well mounted and able to out-distance them. They lost him after a short chase.

But McCracken and Rankin had not failed to score. To add to the discomforts of hunger and weariness, Jim now had an ugly wound from McCracken's rifle across one side of his chest. The bullet did not pass beneath the ribs, but plowed a deep, long furrow through the flesh. It was a painful wound, and within a few days became so infected that it was imperative that he find medication.

As for Deputy McCracken, he was bitterly disappointed that he had failed to bring down the man at whom he had shot, for he was certain that it was McKinney. McCracken, to quote one of his friends, "feared no man on this earth" and liked nothing better than a manhunt, especially if there was hope of a rich reward. When McKinney was finally bagged, the unhealed wound across his chest was to prove to McCracken's fellow deputies that he had not missed his mark, and

• 151

was taken as mute testimony of how close McCracken and Rankin came to collecting the reward.

Canebrake Spring, a familiar camping place for miners and teamsters traveling across Walker Pass to the Kern River, was the scene of many shootings in the early days. Had McCracken aimed an inch or two more accurately, two Bakersfield peace officers might have lived to a ripe old age.

After the incident on the pass, the posses centered their efforts on the White River country, across the pass from Kernville on the western side of the Sierra Divide. It was an old mining community and once possessed the quaint name of Tailholt. As a relic of the Gold Rush days it possessed a Boot Hill cemetery to prove its virility.

On April 13, the *Visalia Times* declared, "McKinney is certainly very close run, and it is hoped he will be captured before another day goes by."

The next day the *Times* reported the outlaw had been seen at Isabella on foot, headed toward Greenhorn Pass. Templeman, Wells, Bly and Piema of the Arizona posse were resting briefly at Randsburg. The *Bakersfield Echo* reported that J. P. Carroll, a celebrated journalist who had represented the *San Francisco Call* in the Evans and Sontag affair, had arrived at Kernville to cover the story for the *San Francisco Examiner*. With him was Lee Wright, a Kansas City newspaper reporter. McKinney had achieved sufficient stature as a colorful Wild West badman to attract the best.

"They intend to be at the front when the news is obtained on the spot," wrote the *Echo* reporter with a hint that his editor would send him to Kernville, too. Among those who looked for McKinney at White River but failed to find him there were the new Bakersfield city marshal and his deputy and best friend, Will Tibbet, a spirited young man who, like Jeff, came from one of Bakersfield's pioneer families. Will, who was married and had several children, was popular in Bakersfield. He had courage, and had demonstrated it as a hard-riding posseman on raids on cattle rustlers in the Kern hills on several occasions.

On April 15, the *Times* reported Jake McKinney had passed through Visalia on his way to Porterville, it being necessary to go to the rail junction at Goshen before making connections to Porterville. A couple of days later he was interviewed by a Visalia reporter and declared that his brother was innocent of the Arizona killings. Jake declined to speculate on his brother's whereabouts.

Sheriff Kelly would have much enjoyed making the pinch on the notorious outlaw at this particular time, for it would have taken the heat off another story that was getting considerable attention in the Bakersfield newspapers. Kelly had been elected on a reform platform and was expected to curb at least to some degree the vice that was rampant in the community. Gambling and prostitution were so wide open and efficiently promoted that they became a hindrance to the development of the oil fields. Kelly had closed up some of the hot spots outside of Bakersfield, for which he won a vote of confidence from the Women's Christian Temperance Union, but he had earned the strong opposition of the worst of the vice element, who feared he would ruin the pleasures and profits.

This large and powerful group set out to discredit Kelly, trumping up a charge that the sheriff, in transporting a prisoner to San Quentin prison, had used his railroad pass to get a free ride and had then illegally entered an expense claim for his fare with the county. The *Californian* treated with ridicule this flimsy attempt to sabotage the reputation of a public official who was only trying to do what his constituents had elected him to do, but Kelly was annoyed. He was well pleased when, early in April, the day of trial arrived, but it could not be held, as his accuser and the chief witness against him failed to appear in court. The judge dismissed the case as being without foundation.

As most of McKinney's troubles had happened on Sunday, it was in keeping with precedent that his wounding by McCracken should have occurred on Sunday, April 12. The next day he took refuge with Jim Dunlap and other friends in the Linn Valley country. The possemen were close on his trail, and he was in great need of food, rest, and time to let his wound heal.

Packard and Tibbet, back in Bakersfield after their trip to the mountains, told a story of having almost trapped McKinney at Dunlap's cabin. They were so close to him that they found a fire blazing on the hearth and fresh food at the table, which was set for two, but no one was around when they broke in. At the corral near the cabin, there was evidence that a horse had been there only minutes before.

The narrow escapes he had had in the mountains convinced McKinney that his best chance for safety lay in the towns, where his friends could offer shelter and keep him informed of the movements of his pursuers. He resolved to go to Bakersfield to obtain not only the rest he sorely needed, but medication for his wound, which was badly festered. In Bakersfield, he reckoned, he might relax in comparative security while he made plans to escape into old Mexico. Other factors, no doubt, helped to influence his decision. He was accepted among the Chinese and could disguise himself as one of them.

The factors which influenced his decision were not to matter to him as he started the last leg of his remarkable 450 miles of flight across some of America's most rugged country.

•
•   •   •
•   •   •

IX

IT WAS never made quite clear in the newspaper accounts of McKinney's last flight how he covered the final 35 or 40 miles from Linn Valley to Bakersfield, but it is highly probable that he went on foot. A walking man is less conspicuous than one on horseback and better able to hide when approached on the road. The outlaw had been given little chance to rest and recuperate his strength in the mountains, and it must have been with a great sense of relief when he covered the final miles of his flight to Bakersfield. There he had the anticipation of a haven among his own kind, with medicine for his wound and narcotics to ease the pain. He still had money from the Blakey-Winchester murder and robbery in his pocket, and in Bakersfield there would be the opportunity to find more to help him get to Mexico.

He reached Bakersfield near dusk on Thursday, April 16, and lurked in the outskirts until darkness fell. He then made his way to the cemetery just east of town, where he hid his prized shotguns and two rifles in some brush and weeds near the roadside.

It is very likely that before leaving Linn Valley he arranged a rendezvous with Jake and others at the cemetery, for it was common talk later that Jake and another man had brought Jim into Bakersfield hidden under a blanket in the back of a wagon. It is also probable that arrangements had been made to hide him in the room of Al Hulse, his friend of Merced days, who was now a tinhorn gambler, erstwhile deputy constable, pimp, ruffian, and narcotics user in the Bakersfield tenderloin. Hulse was later to deny that the shelter he gave the outlaw was pre-arranged. He contended it was a spur-of-the-moment decision reached after he was approached by his old friend, McKinney, on a dark street on the night of April 16.

Al was staying at the Chinese joss house on L Street. His room mate, when she was not engaged in the practice of her profession, was an unyouthful, dark-eyed beauty of the Bakersfield half-world who called herself Jenny Fox. She and Al were good customers of the opium den located in the cellar below their room. In addition to being well known to the Oriental peddlers of narcotics, Hulse was also said to be a member of the ruffian fraternity referred to as the Chinese Masons, to which a membership had also been extended to Jim McKinney.

On Friday night, Hulse brought several of McKinney's friends to the joss house to confer with the outlaw, and the immediate problem being the arrangement of details for the flight to Mexico, it was decided that McKinney should remain in Bakersfield no longer than was necessary for the infection in his wound to subside. Jim's brothers, Ed and Jake, were among the visitors. They were continuing negotiations to bring about a truce between the Arizona sheriff, Lovin, and Jim in hope that a fair hearing would clear Jim of the Arizona murders. There seems to be no truth in later rumors that the negotiations were about to bear fruit, and had McKinney been given more time, he would have surrendered peacefully.

Jake and Ed left town the day before the final battle, apparently with the intent of drawing off the pursuit. Jake went to Porterville and Ed to Lathrop, 250 miles away. But the red herring they were attempting to draw across the trail failed to distract Jim's enemies.

Some time Friday Hulse went to a drug store and purchased a bottle of carbolic acid, remarking to the druggist that he wanted an antiseptic for the treatment of a gunshot wound, whose he did not say.

On Friday evening, Hulse went to a livery stable and hired a rig in which he and McKinney drove out to the cemetery. In the darkness they had some difficulty in finding McKinney's guns. Still later, they went to a restaurant in the tenderloin and, choosing a table in a dimly lighted corner, ate a meal.

Dave Moshier and Art Kilbreth came down by train from Porterville and met McKinney in the restaurant. It is probable that Dave, who was one of McKinney's confidants, came to the restaurant by previous arrangement to meet the outlaw, but Art, who had a few days off from work, accompanied Moshier to Bakersfield without knowing the purpose of the trip. The restaurant in which the meeting took place was operated by Kilbreth's mother-in-law.

Kilbreth, who had last seen McKinney on the night of the trouble in Porterville, was struck by the appearance of the outlaw. He was thin and worn, his neat moustache was gone, and he appeared to be frightened as he skulked in the dark corner of the room. McKinney was seated with a man Kilbreth did not recognize, and Kilbreth exchanged a few cautious words with the badman before hurrying away to avoid drawing attention.

On Saturday, McKinney's friends met with him in the joss house room again while Hulse set about the errands most important to arranging for the flight to Mexico. He was to obtain ammunition for McKinney's guns and purchase a suitable horse on which Jim could make the trip. The shotgun and rifle ammunition he obtained at a hardware store. Later admission of this purchase was to be one of the bits of evidence responsible for his conviction on charges of being an accomplice of McKinney in the killings which were to occur the following day.

After purchasing the ammunition, Hulse went to a livery stable and hired a rig. He picked up Jenny Fox at the joss house and the two set off for the country to buy a saddle horse.

Albert S. Goode, who was to become one of Kern County's most prominent dairymen, was riding out toward his dairy in the Rosedale district Saturday morning when he met Hulse and Jenny in the buggy. They were having considerable trouble attempting to lead a spirited saddle horse behind the rig. Hulse, who was acquainted with Goode, stopped him and offered him $20 to take the horse to the Lon Davis livery stable in Bakersfield. Goode declined the money but offered to deliver the horse as a favor. He took the lead rope and found the horse would follow behind his own mount with no trouble.

It was late in the afternoon when Goode finished his duties at the dairy and started back to town. At Kern River he met Hulse much concerned, headed for Rosedale. He demanded to know why Goode had not delivered the horse as he had promised. Goode explained that he had thought there was no hurry and had finished his work before starting back to town to deliver the horse.

Hulse had purchased the horse from George Coffey, a rancher, who made the deal entirely without the knowledge that its intended use was for McKinney's escape into Mexico. It was an excellent animal. Goode was convinced that with such an animal under him, McKinney could have kept well ahead of pursuit and by following little known trails through the mountains

● 161

and desert south of Bakersfield and by skirting Imperial Valley could have made his escape across the border. The next day Goode was delivering milk just two blocks from the joss house when he heard the shots of the fatal battle. For his innocent act of accommodation to Hulse in delivering the horse, he was waited on later by a group of Sheriff Kelly's men and was made to give a concise accounting for his actions of the previous day. He was told that only his reputation kept him from being arrested as an accomplice of McKinney and Hulse.

Among those who visited the joss house on Saturday was Dave Ingram, proprietor of a saloon at Isabella. Four months before Dave had been absolved of the killing of a Mexican miner at his place of business on the grounds of self defense. The Mexican had tried to assault Ingram with a quart bottle of whiskey as a weapon and Ingram, badly beaten around the head, was forced to draw his six-shooter and plug the miner.

The joss house on L Street stood on the east side of the street, midway between 21st and 22nd Streets. It served as a religious shrine, clubhouse, lodging house, and headquarters for the Oriental members of a tong. The building was a two-story affair, narrow and ugly, with wooden awnings extending over the sidewalk from the first floor. Butting up against the south side of the joss house was a Chinese general merchandise store and along the north side ran a narrow alley. Across the alley to the north was a building occupied by Sing Lee, one of the elder statesmen or patriarchs of Bakersfield's numerous Chinese population. He operated, along with his legitimate businesses, a highly profitable lottery.

East and north of the joss house stretched a series of squalid shacks occupied by Chinese laundries, stores and restaurants, many of which were merely fronts for opium dens which were operated in the cellars.

Across L Street to the west was a respectable working-men's boarding house operated by Mrs. Charles Duval. The front housed a bar.

Along L Street to the south was a succession of saloons, restaurants and pleasure palaces, among them the Owl dance hall, a noisy place which usually stayed open all night; the Palace, Salcedo's, the White, and the Silver saloons. On the corner of 19th and L Streets was Tom Owens' gambling hall, the largest in Bakersfield, marking the southern limit of the tenderloin. West of the gambling hall, on the same side of the street, was the Reception Saloon, at the rear of which McKinney had killed Red Sears two years before and where Hulse was to claim he was placidly watching a card game when McKinney made his last stand.

Located in the variegated scene of gaiety, sin and tragedy which was Bakersfield's tenderloin, the joss house was divided inside into a cellar, first floor, and second floor. The cellar ran under the entire building and had two entrances, one by means of a stairway leading down from the sidewalk at the front of the building, and the other by means of steps which led down from the interior of the building next to the rear door. One portion of the basement contained the rows of bunks in which those partaking of the smoke of the poppy might relax to enjoy their dreams. It was commonly believed by the white population of Bakersfield

• 163

that all basements in Chinatown were connected by tunnels into a sinister, labyrinthian underworld where the mysterious Orientals practiced their strange vices safe from the prying disapproval of Occidentals.

The front portion of the first floor of the joss house contained the traditional shrine, a beautiful work of art of intricate carving and bright lacquered colors. Behind the room containing the shrine was a series of small rooms opening off a central, narrow hall. The rear room on the north side contained a small kitchen. The room next to it was used as a dining room and club room by the Chinese inhabitants. Across the hall from the kitchen was the room occupied by Al Hulse and in which he hid McKinney. Little is remembered of the layout of the second floor, and it is not important to the story. Presumably it was devoted entirely to sleeping rooms for Chinese.

Behind the joss house was a small rear yard perhaps thirty feet wide, extending back from the building for about twenty feet. It was enclosed by a high board fence which had no opening onto the alley. Access to the outside was through a narrow wooden gate opening on the south side of the enclosure.

Inside the yard near the rear door of the joss house and to the right of the gate as one entered was a wooden outhouse divided into two sections, each having its own door. The side nearest the gate contained the urinal.

Around this strange, ugly joss house was to occur on Sunday morning, April 19, 1903, Bakersfield's most sensational act of violence, the final stand of the last badman of the Old West.

On Saturday night, August 18, Al Hulse, the debauched stonecutter, stepped into the Reception Saloon on 19th Street to have a few drinks to lighten the strenuous responsibilities of the day. As in every saloon in that part of California, the pursuit of Jim McKinney was the principal topic of conversation along the bar, and the possibility that the outlaw might even then be in Bakersfield lent a tension to the atmosphere. Hulse, bursting with the intimacy of his association with the subject so much discussed, could not resist the temptation to boast.

"Jim McKinney," he confided with certainty to the boys along the bar, "isn't more than 300 yards from this very spot."

X

$\mathbb{E}$PIC EVENTS in the history of a community live in the memories of contemporary citizens through association with personal experiences. Just as nearly every adult American can tell unhesitatingly what he was doing the Sunday morning the Japanese hit Pearl Harbor, Bakersfield citizens old enough to remember can detail their activities of that Sunday morning in 1903 when the town marshal and his deputy were mortally wounded and the infamous outlaw, McKinney, met his fate.

Lawrence Weill, one of Bakersfield's most prominent business figures, never forgot that he was waiting his turn in a barber shop just a few blocks away when the shooting started and arrived at the joss house before the wounded had been removed. In later years he was taken on a tour of the building by Burt Tibbet. Charlie Owens missed the excitement, having left early that morning to go fishing on the Kern River. Jesse Dorsey, who for half a century and more was to represent Kern County in the state legislature, was working in his law office when he heard the commotion. He was well acquainted with McKinney and Hulse, the latter having only recently served as an important defense witness in a trial in which Dorsey successfully defended a little colored woman for the killing of her brutal husband. George Hudson, who later was to patrol a beat in the Bakersfield tenderloin as a policeman, hopped on his bicycle on hearing the news of the battle and on his way to the scene passed the buggy in which the wounded marshal, Packard, was being transported to his home. Albert Goode, as previously stated, was peddling milk just two blocks away and paid little attention to the gunfire until he saw others hastening in that direction. Lemon Paul heard the shots at his home four blocks to the east, but prudently decided against verifying his suspicion that violence was once more having its inning and Bakersfield was having a surfeit of men for late Sunday breakfast.

All those who recall the day are still impressed by the rapidity with which the news of the fight spread across the city. "They've got McKinney cornered in the joss house and he is shooting them all dead," was the terrifying report heard up and down the streets.

While this flying rumor was hardly true, it was as close to the facts as were a number of other stories which were broadcast that day. To this time, fantastic stories in connection with the battle are accepted as truth. Yet it is not difficult to arrive somewhere near the true course of events if one takes the trouble to read the transcript of the coroner's inquest, the newspaper accounts, and the records of the two subsequent trials of Al Hulse. Of all these, the records of the coroner seem to tell the most logical story. In the great sheaf of papers from the inquest lies proof that Hulse missed his calling. He should have been an attorney.

Coroner S. D. Mullins impaneled a jury composed of very prominent citizens, including W. R. Coons, Jess Minter, E. M. Roberts, Lon Davis, George Haberfelde, William Tyler, J. S. Drury and M. A. Duncan. He called them together April 22, three days after the tragedy, but the session was not held as planned because Sheriff Kelly was occupied with a new shooting which had occurred in connection with a quarrel over an oil lease. Other important witnesses and members of the blue-ribbon jury wanted a postponement so that they might attend the funerals of the two brave peace officers who had lost their lives.

"There was a great many people around there that day," said George Fluornoy, who represented the district attorney at the inquest. "Some saw this and some saw that."

He wanted everyone present who could offer something of importance to the proceedings. Al Hulse, who was in jail fighting as fine a case of narcotics-withdrawal hallucinations as his fellow prisoners had ever seen, was in no shape to be present until several days had elapsed, and he was the one most vitally interested in the inquest testimony.

On April 30, eleven days after the fight, Coroner Mullins managed to put together the first day of the inquest, and with Sheriff Kelly as the first witness, the events of the tragic Sunday began to take shape.

Kelly related how Sheriff Lovin arrived by train in Bakersfield from Randsburg at seven o'clock that fatal morning, and Kelly and City Marshal Packard met him at the station. There Packard told the two sheriffs he had information that Al Hulse had boasted the night before that McKinney was not more than a couple of blocks away from the Reception Saloon, and that other bits of information had been picked up to corroborate Hulse's statement that McKinney was in town. Packard also disclosed that he had been negotiating with Ed McKinney for a meeting with the outlaw but had not been able to reach an agreement with Ed on the terms of surrender.

Having seen the bodies of the two men McKinney had so brutally slain in Arizona, Sheriff Lovin was against giving the outlaw any kind of consideration. He advised Packard and Kelly that he believed the best course of procedure would be to organize a posse and bring the matter to a showdown with no delay.

Although Packard did not know for certain that McKinney was holed up at the joss house, the peace officers decided it would be the most likely place to explore first, for they knew that Hulse was rooming there and that he was closely associated with the outlaw.

170 •

About nine o'clock, Kelly and Packard began gathering a posse. Packard, who seemed younger than his forty years, had contempt for the outlaw and supreme confidence in his own courage and ability. Jeff had been on manhunts before and had been more than a match for the roughest of the characters who had broken the law in his town. For his partner in the showdown with Jim McKinney, he again selected his friend, Will Tibbet, a man Packard knew to be possessed of courage to match his own and one who would not run from a fight.

The two men were much alike. Both were from families which stood high in respectability from pioneer days. Both loved excitement. Jeff and Will were acquainted with and respected by most of the characters of the tenderloin. They had hunted bear together for the sport of it, and they had been together on more exciting chases in the many wars on cattle rustlers and other evil-doers of the times. Both men were merry-hearted individuals who liked a good time. They were prominent in their lodges and in community enterprises. They were far too busy enjoying life and taking part in the many adventures open to them to absorb any of the riches of the vast oil development so prominent about them.

Neither Jeff nor Will was big in stature, but both were athletic in build with an air of physical efficiency about them. Packard wore thick lensed glasses to correct myopia and was seldom seen without a well chewed cigar in his mouth. Tibbet was a fancy dresser. As a peace officer, he went in for show. He wore two big six-shooters in holsters on his hips and topped off his western costume with an expensive "ten-gallon" Stetson hat. Both Jeff and Will were expert horsemen and were marksmen with rifle and pistol.

Others chosen as members of the posse were men who were known to be dependable in an emergency. Deputy Sheriff Burt Tibbet, brother of Will, was much like his brother but of quieter disposition. Deputies Tom Baker and Frank (Gus) Tower had ridden with Kelly into the desert in search of McKinney and deserved another chance at the outlaw. Packard drafted another member of his staff, Deputy Marshal Ernest Etter. Sheriff Collins of Tulare County was in Bakersfield in anticipation of the capture of the outlaw and he, at the invitation of Sheriff Kelly, became a member of the posse.

The posse held a rendezvous at the jail where it was ascertained that all had, in addition to their hand guns, rifles or shotguns in the event the anticipated fight at close quarters became a reality. Packard had a rifle. Will and Burt Tibbet had shotguns.

The posse left the jail about 10:30, traveling in three horse drawn vehicles. Packard and Will Tibbet rode in Packard's buggy and Lovin and Collins accompanied Sheriff Kelly in his buggy. The rest of the deputies climbed aboard a horse-drawn bus which was part of the sheriff's equipment. In order not to attract attention, each vehicle took a separate route to a rendezvous at the rear of the Duval boarding house, across L Street west of the joss house, where the officers held another council to decide on their strategy.

Packard, still confident that if he could manage to come face to face with the outlaw he could persuade him to give up without a fight, volunteered to search the joss house. His companion of many manhunts, Will Tibbet, asked to accompany him. Perhaps Jeff was thinking of the times he had befriended McKinney, even helping to put up money for Jim's bail after the slaying of Tom Sears. Perhaps he was thinking that he could save the outlaw's life if he reached him before the vindictive Arizona sheriff, who had forcefully expressed his opinion against sparing the outlaw. Sheriff Kelly was reluctant to permit the two men to expose themselves to a known killer who had made his boast to "kill anyone who looks at me," but Bakersfield was Packard's jurisdiction, and Kelly was not in command. It was up to Packard to take the lead.

As Jeff and Will prepared for their part of the search, Kelly stationed the others of the posse at strategic points. Burt Tibbet took his place in the alley on the north side of the boarding house with a good view of the joss house across the street. Kelly remained behind the boarding house in a position to cover the action either to the north or south. Tower took a round-about route, so that he might not be seen, to a point of vantage in the alley at the rear of the joss house, with Etter a short distance ahead of him. Lovin went to the corner of 21st and L Streets, taking a position of prominence because he was not known in Bakersfield and would not arouse suspicion of anyone who might pass him on the street. Sheriff Collins drifted down 21st Street a

• 173

short distance so that he might cover the rear of the joss house from the south.

From these points of vantage the posse members watched as Packard and Tibbet, once again in their buggy, made a circuit of the block and stopped in front of the joss house and, otherwise conducting themselves as if they were on routine business, took their time in tying up their team. Their companions on the stake-out saw them slip quietly down the stairway to the basement and disappear. Thus the stage was set from the side of law enforcement for this last big gun battle of the Old West.

To set the stage from the outlaw's side is not so easy. Jenny Fox was the only one to testify from that viewpoint at the coroner's inquest, and she was later to impeach her own testimony. In the perspective of a half a century or more, her first story seems most logical, despite the fact that she later repudiated it.

Jenny was a prostitute by profession and the consort of Al Hulse during the days he sheltered McKinney. She was referred to in the newspapers accounts as "the French woman," a nationality which was all too often applied to women of her profession, warranted or not. Lemon Paul, himself part French and conversant in five languages, once addressed her in French and she did not answer. He switched to Spanish and received a fluent reply. Jenny was to become a major figure in the aftermath of the shooting, and she caught the interest of Bakersfield as the woman in the case.

Jenny was notorious not only in Bakersfield, but over most of Arizona as well. She had worked in most of the raucous mining camps of the territory and it is a safe bet that she was among the more than 500 prostitutes who registered in a single year in Tombstone when her trade was legalized and regulated by license and medical examination. She had plied her trade in Kingman and no doubt was known to Jim McKinney during the time he hid out near that community.

She was typical of her kind, one of the dance hall girls for whose favors the miners, often isolated from feminine companionship for weeks and months at a time, would gladly pay.

"After weeks of hard work in some mine a hundred miles from nowhere," said one old miner. "it was something just to sit down and talk to a woman, any kind of a woman. We just did not have time to meet the good ones, so we took the ones whose time we could buy. They generally had all your money before they were through with you, but they'd usually grubstake you back to the mine or help you find another job."

Jenny's kind were completely without standing, the untouchables, figuratively but not literally, in their society. One of the unwritten rules of the profession was not to recognize in public any man with whom they had been intimate in private, unless they were first acknowledged by the man.

Like the cowboys of the time, each prostitute acquired a "handle" to her name, usually descriptive in a suggestive or just plain lewd sort of way. Big-Nose Kate, Horizontal Hannah, Bow-Legged Beulah, French Mary, One Dollar Winnie, and Spanish Rosie are typical examples. Jenny was known throughout Arizona as

• 175

Pissin' Jenny, significant of her usual first act after turning a trick. She was a buxom woman, built to handle
twenty, thirty, or more customers a night when the occasion demanded, without weariness. She was the rugged peasant type, probably of Slavic origin, a handsome woman of dark features who spoke with a slight
accent. She was forty years old or more when she witnessed the fight in the joss house, and she still had mile-
age left in her. Hers was a sturdy constitution to survive for so many years the booze, dope and disease
common to her profession.

Jenny's story of what happened in Hulse's room the
night before the shooting was corroborated in part later
by Hulse, but as he denied being in the room when the
battle took place, he could not help but deny that a
portion of Jenny's story was true.

It appears that Saturday night was spent by McKinney in conference with a number of men who came to
help him plan his get-away, or possibly for friendly, if
somewhat hazardous and ill-advised, visits. Jenny recalled seeing several men come and go, but she paid
little attention to their identity although she admitted
she was in the room much of the time.

Jenny told the inquest jury that she left the room
about two o'clock in the morning to go to the cellar to
smoke opium. About 10 o'clock in the morning she
came back to the room to "get her clothing." In the
room she saw Hulse, McKinney, and a third man, the
latter a well-dressed individual who wore a dark suit
and a white hat. She did not recognize him. McKinney
was seated on the floor and the other two men were on

176 •

the bed. Jenny herself took a place on the bed, back against the wall away from the center of the group. On a small table in the room were bread, butter, and other food. As evidence of the autopsy was to show later, McKinney had breakfasted well. There were a good many guns close at hand—rifles, shotguns, and revolvers, according to Jenny's recollection.

This, according to Jenny Fox, was the setting for the battle from the outlaw's side.

Hulse was to consistently deny Jenny's contention that he was in the room when the trouble started. He was to tell how he arose early Sunday morning, leaving McKinney in the room. His version was that he went to a barber shop where he saw and conversed with Deputy Marshal Etter. From there he went to the Reception Saloon and was watching a card game when the gun battle occurred.

The movements of Packard and Tibbet from the time they entered the joss house must be traced piecemeal from fragments of conversation Dr. Shafer remembered having had with Packard as he treated his wounds and from what Burt Tibbet could recall of Packard's account to him when he visited the dying man at the Packard home the afternoon following the shooting

Jeff and Will first moved carefully through the opium den in the cellar, checking the bunks. They then went to the first floor by way of the rear stairs and began checking the rooms on each side of the hall. In most of the rooms they found only Chinese who, under questioning, feigned ignorance of English or denied having

● 177

seen any white person in the place. The door to the room at the rear of the joss house, on the south side of the hall, was locked, and there was no response to their knock. Determined to have a look inside the room, Packard went in search of a Chinese who might have a key to the door, but could find no one to help him.

Packard came back to the door where Tibbet was waiting, and the two decided to try a skeleton key Tibbet carried on his key ring. In order to work at the lock with both hands, Tibbet set the butt of his shotgun on the floor and leaned the weapon up against the wall. Packard held his rifle across his body to cover the door when it opened. No trained peace officer today would so approach a door behind which a deadly gunman might be lurking, but raw courage, rather than a knowledge of police methods, was the chief asset of the frontier lawmen.

Inside the room, according to Jenny Fox, the occupants heard Packard and Tibbet talking outside and immediately tensed. They heard a voice demand to know who was in the room, and they heard a Chinese accent reply that he did not know. There was a pause of a minute or two, and then they heard a key turning the lock.

"We're in for it," McKinney quietly told his companions.

"Let's go," said Hulse.

With that, they picked up weapons, one a rifle and the other a shotgun—it was never quite determined which had which—and aimed at the door. The third man in the room did not arm himself, according to

178 •

Jenny, but remained on the bed. McKinney took a stance squarely in front of the door. Hulse remained behind and to one side of McKinney.

As the door was thrown open from the outside, Jenny watched only the firing of the first shots before jumping between the bed and the wall and flinging herself to the floor.

There was a deafening discharge of guns reverberating in the little room. In pauses in the uproar, Jenny heard the excited, high pitched voice of Jim McKinney.

"There goes old Four-Eyes," he exulted, obviously referring to Packard, who always wore glasses, as the marshal tumbled backward from the onslaught of shot and bullets.

"And there goes old Overall," shouted McKinney, mistaking Tibbet for his old enemy, the former sheriff of Tulare County whom he knew to be active in the hunt for him.

"Let's go for Gus," Jenny heard McKinney say to Hulse as the two men stepped through the doorway into the hall. Jenny fled from the room and could offer no more eye-witness testimony. She entered a closet to hide and someone locked the door behind her.

Packard's account of the fight as told to Dr. Shafer before the marshal died indicated that Jeff and Will were taken quite by surprise. As the door swung open after Will succeeded in unlocking it, Packard saw McKinney standing squarely in the center of the room, his shotgun to his shoulder and trained on Tibbet.

"Look out, Bill, he has got you," Packard cried out, at the same time throwing his rifle to his shoulder and

● 179

pulling the trigger. Simultaneously with the crash of the gun's discharge, Packard felt his right hand and arm grow numb and drop uncontrollably to his side. As he tried to bring the arm back into use and cock his rifle, the roar of gunfire at pointblank range almost burst his eardrums and he felt his left arm become useless. The rifle clattered on the floor. "Then," he told Dr. Shafer, "I was blown right out of the house."

Packard was literally overwhelmed with rifle and shotgun fire. The plucky peace officer, as the evidence of bullet marks on the opposite wall was to show, managed to fire his heavy rifle twice, but his aim was spoiled by counterfire. It was brought out in the investigation that the bullet from a rifle in the hands of someone in the room had struck the end of Packard's rifle, knocking off the sight. A portion of the bullet actually entered the barrel of Packard's gun, so that when he discharged it the recoil was strong enough to force the wounded man backward and he fell out the rear door.

Poor Will Tibbet never fired a shot.

With a gaping wound from a rifle bullet in his right side and buckshot wounds in his hands and face, Will staggered through the rear door and collapsed at the foot of the steps.

But the fight was not over, and McKinney was not destined to enjoy for long the fruits of his temporary victory. Outside were many courageous men, among them Will's brother, Burt, who were not afraid of a gun fight.

Burt, from his position in the alley beside Mrs. Duval's boarding house, heard the shooting start and immediately ran down the alley, crossing L Street. As fast as he could run he headed for the rear of the joss house, where the shots seemed to be concentrated. As he passed the rear window of the building, he saw Deputy Etter firing his revolver through the window.

Burt ran around the fenced rear yard to the gate on the south side. "Come on in, you fellows! Come on in," he heard Packard call.

Burt jumped through the gate to see Packard standing, weaponless, in the doorway of the urinal side of the outhouse, his arms dangling uselessly at his sides and blood running off his fingers.

The door to the other compartment of the outhouse was closed, and Burt levelled his shotgun at it.

"No, no," shouted Packard, motioning with his head toward the rear door of the joss house.

"Look out! He's in the door!"

Burt whirled and looked at the rear door of the joss house in time to see the barrel of McKinney's shotgun poked through the crack of the partly opened door. Then the outlaw stuck his head part way out to get a cautious look.

At almost pointblank range, not more than a dozen feet separating them, the two men stared down the murderous barrels of their shotguns for a vital instant.

Tibbet was first to recover from the momentary surprise both men felt. He fired and McKinney reeled back, falling to the floor and dropping his gun.

"I advanced toward the door and I heard McKinney get up and walk away to the window of the kitchen," Burt said at the inquest.

"He came back again and I saw the barrel of his gun come out the door, then his whole body. He throwed his gun out at me and at that moment I shot him and turned around and saw my brother lying there. Etter came in and led Packard out and Tower came in to where McKinney's body was."

Burt Tibbet's second shot had been fired at a range of less than six feet.

Will Tibbet was lying on his side a foot or two from the back door. Burt bent over and removed his brave brother's gun belt.

"Bill, are you shot?" Burt asked.

"Yes," groaned Will. "Let me turn over."

"Who shot you?" Burt queried.

"Hulse shot me," was the reply, according to Burt's sworn testimony.

Burt stated at the inquest that as he talked with his brother he could hear footsteps receding down the hall of the joss house. He was convinced that these were the footsteps of Al Hulse.

Tower, who had been in the alley back of the joss house, ran toward the source of the shots as he heard them. He arrived outside the north kitchen window in time to see the badman run toward the window after receiving Burt Tibbet's first blast of shot. Tower fired his rifle quickly through the window but missed. However, he forced McKinney to retreat to the rear door once more where Burt was ready with a second, and fatal shotgun blast. Tower ran around the fence to the gate and entered to find Burt crouched solicitously

182 •

over his brother. Tower ran past the brothers and burst through the joss house door.

"Look out. He may have four or five friends in there," Burt called to him as he passed.

Tower dashed into the kitchen and heard a scramble of footsteps ahead of him. He caught a glimpse of a fleeing figure passing through a door leading into the connecting room. A mush pot crashed from the stove to the floor, as if it had been upset and knocked off by someone passing in haste. Tower stepped cautiously through the door into the adjoining room but saw only "four or five cowering Chinamen." He then went to the room where the fight had started, but found no one. He also made a quick search of the cellar. There was no one there.

Deputy Tower ceased his hazardous prowling and returned to the hallway inside the back door where the rear stairway to the cellar led downward. McKinney's body was draped precariously over the flimsy railing which protected the narrow entrance to the cellar. Tower flung the body to the floor and removed a .44 caliber Smith & Wesson revolver from McKinney's belt. He also picked up a 10-gauge shotgun from the floor near the body. He pulled the body out the rear door, as it was blocking access to the hallway.

McKinney had died instantly from the second shot. The first had torn a gaping hole in the side of his neck. The second blasted away most of the left side of his face and several shot entered his brain near the side of the left ear.

• 183

Tower recovered a .25-.35 caliber rifle and a smaller rifle from Hulse's room. The heavy weapon showed signs of considerable recent use. Tower checked McKinney's shotgun. It had been fired and reloaded. McKinney's six-shooter was fully loaded and was clean, indicating it had not been used in the battle.

A later check was to show that 32 rounds of rifle, shotgun, and revolver shots had been fired in the exchange between peace officers and badmen in the battle.

XI

Jim McKinney, the notorious outlaw, was dead, but the excitement of his passing and the sensational events which were to be appended to it had scarcely begun. The newspapers were to revel in a yarn which had a new lead for every edition. That Sunday was to be one Bakersfield would never forget, and the story was to remain fresh for three years more, to end in a final, sordid, gruesome suicide in a lonely cell in the Bakersfield jail.

When the last shot was expended in the gun battle, Burt Tibbet and Tower were convinced that Hulse was still in the joss house and perhaps others of McKinney's friends as well, in a killing mood and ready to make a last stand rather than be taken alive. Sheriff Kelly had already lost enough men and did not propose to risk more by sending them into the dark recesses of a building which had proved to be a death trap.

If Hulse was in the building, and no has ever seriously considered that he was not, he made a remarkable escape. If there was still a third man in that fatal room and he was not just a figment of Jenny's opium dreams, he made an even more remarkable exit from the scene.

The more urgent business after the shooting was to get the sorely wounded peace officers out of the area of danger and to places where they might receive medical attention. Will Tibbet's brother and fellow officers moved him in Packard's buggy to Baer's Drug Store at 19th and Chester, three blocks away, and there a crowd gathered to get a glimpse of him as he lay on the floor, writhing with pain. Packard, apparently less critically wounded, was taken in Sheriff Kelly's buggy several blocks to the Packard home on 18th Street.

Will, suffering greatly, was later removed to the Southern Hotel for surgery, as Bakersfield, for all its wealth, had no hospital. Before he was removed from the drug store, his aged mother visited him and a tender deathbed scene between mother and son ensued, for Will told her he knew he was not to survive. Ed Tibbet, another brother, arrived in time to perform that last meaningful rite common to men of the Old West; at Will's request, Ed removed his brother's shoes, that he might not die with them on.

Dr. C. W. Kellogg, Dr. S. F. Smith and Dr. J. L. Carson were summoned to attend Tibbet. The wound in

186 •

his right side was made by a steel jacketed rifle bullet which had virtually destroyed the right kidney. Will's right hand bore a severe wound made by shotgun pellets, and he also had two shotgun pellets in his face.

The doctors could do nothing for him. He died at 12:19 o'clock, less than two hours after he was shot and before surgery could be started.

Dr. Shafer and Dr. Taggart attended Packard. He had a massive flesh wound in the lower jaw inflicted by a jagged fragment of a rifle bullet torn off when the missile struck the barrel of Packard's own gun. The fragment had passed down into his neck. He was severely wounded in both hands by buckshot and had a flesh wound from a rifle bullet on his hip. His most serious wound, however, was that apparently made by a bullet which had struck his left forearm, shattering the bone so badly that a portion of it had to be removed by surgery that afternoon. As Dr. Shafer removed the wounded man's shirt, he found the bullet which had made the arm wound. It had passed through Jeff's coat and was lodged against a wallet he carried in his inside coat pocket.

Despite the number of Packard's wounds, Packard did not appear to be fatally hurt. After working over him most of the afternoon, Dr. Shafer left him in the care of a nurse. Jeff was in good spirits and talked freely. He received such visitors as Dr. Shafer admitted, including Burt Tibbet and Sheriff Kelly. He told Dr. Shafer and Tibbet of the events in the joss house leading up to the shooting and declared he knew

Hulse had been in the room, although he did not specifically mention seeing him as he did McKinney. About five o'clock the next morning, the nurse put in a hurried call for Dr. Shafer. When he arrived at the Packard home, he found that his patient had slipped into a profound coma as the result of shock. Despite all that Dr. Shafer could do, Jeff died an hour later. The physician, who could not believe that the wounds were primarily responsible for the death, asked for and received permission to do an autopsy. He determined that Jeff, while he had appeared to be in excellent health, was suffering from both heart and liver conditions which made it impossible for him to survive the shock of his wounds.

Jeff had the solace of his wife's presence in his dying hours. Will Tibbet's wife, Ellen, did not reach his side before he died, and neither did their small children, among them a little boy, Lawrence, who was to grow up to gain fame in opera and the cinema, and who would one day relate the story of his valiant father's passing on a television show.

McKinney's body, followed by a crowd of the morbid and curious, was taken to Payne & Hansberger's Mortuary, where it was laid out on a stretcher supported by two sawhorses in the back room among the caskets and scatterings of excelsior used for padding caskets. The coroner found $170 in Jim's pockets, probably the remains of the loot he had obtained from Blakey and Winchester two weeks before. When he took off the dead man's shirt, the coroner noted the festering, encrusted wound across his chest. He lifted off the scab and inspected the wound more closely, deciding in his own mind that McKinney might not have been able to survive the infection had he not obtained medical treatment.

A photographer came in and took pictures of the nude body, a dirty white towel thrown over the loins, to be used in case pictorial evidence was needed later. Jim's thin, emaciated form, with wounds on the neck, chest and once handsome face, was not exactly a pleasant subject for photography.

"Burt, you did a good deed," had been Jeff Packard's last words to Burt Tibbet during their visit in the afternoon. Jim McKinney, shotgun murderer, dead and harmless on a slab, his career of bloodshed ended, was the deed to which Jeff referred.

Removal of the dead and wounded from the scene of conflict did not terminate the excitement at the joss house. Kelly, Lovin and Collins held a council of war and decided that Hulse was probably still in the joss house, ready to make a determined stand, as no one had seen him leave. It was with difficulty that they kept the steadily growing crowd which collected at the scene from pressing too closely to the possible danger of flying bullets. The Chinese occupants had fled, and the building now stood quiet and ominous, with the smell of gunsmoke about it. The three sheriffs talked of setting fire to the building to smoke out the gunman supposedly still inside and the fire department was actually summoned to stand by in the event the plan was put into execution. Fortunately for Jenny Fox this was not done, for, unknown to those outside, she was still in the building, locked securely in the closet into which she had fled after the shooting. Someone suggested that the fire department lay hoses to the cellar and fill it with water, which, if Hulse were hiding in some secret passageway as many suggested, would force him to surface.

Such drastic methods were not to be necessary. As Kelly and his deputy, Tower, rode south on L Street in Kelly's buggy to make arrangements to flood the basement, they were amazed to see Al Hulse step out of a Chinese store near the Palace dance hall a block and a half from the joss house. He walked calmly out into the street to intercept the officers. "I understand you fellows are looking for me," he said to the flabbergasted officers.

He pulled a six-gun from his belt and handed it, butt first, to Kelly and then surrendered a long-bladed hunting knife as he climbed into the buggy. He put on such an air of injured innocence that Kelly and Tower did not even bother to handcuff him as they hustled him off to jail, where he was put away safely in a cell on the second floor.

Returning to the joss house, Kelly ordered a thorough search of the building. Tower broke the locked closet door and hauled out Jenny Fox. Questioned as to her whereabouts during the battle, she defiantly denied having seen anything. Someone had shoved her in the closet and locked the door before it all started, she said. Despite her denials, she was hauled off to jail and booked as a possible accomplice.

If Hulse was a participant in the gun fight, how did he get out of the joss house without someone seeing him?

"Don't get it into your head there was only one man in that room," Packard told Burt Tibbet before he died. "There were certainly more."

Although Packard never said to anyone that he actually saw Hulse in the room, Jeff was obviously convinced beyond a doubt that Hulse was there, and that he was firing a gun. Before Will Tibbet died, he told his brothers, Burt and Ed, that it was Hulse who shot him. Others in the room at Baer's Drug Store at the time heard him make the statement.

The public was willing to believe that Hulse escaped through one of those mysterious tunnels which were supposed to link the sinister Oriental underworlds in the Chinese sections of all cities. The Celestials were said to use these labyrinthian dens of iniquity as a means of taking their pleasure in opium and slave girls undetected. They also used them in their grim and deadly hatchet warfare, according to legend. However, a thorough check of the joss house cellar failed to reveal any such escape route, although the story still exists in Bakersfield today that the Chinese spirited Hulse out of the place by means of a secret passage.

It is obvious that the posse's stake-out of the joss house broke down when the shooting started. The peace officers left their stations to rush to the aid of Packard and Tibbet. It would have been possible in the excitement for Hulse or anyone else to have escaped out the front door and lose himself in the nearby buildings without being observed. It would also have been possible for the wily Hulse to disguise himself as a Chinese and flee with them when they left the place. At Hulse's trial, a witness was introduced who said she had observed the scene from Mrs. Duval's boarding house and had seen a man wearing a distinguishing white hat run out the door. Hulse countered with testimony that Sheriff Lovin wore a white hat that day and was in the vicinity of the front entrance. Hulse was to steadfastly stick by his story that he was watching a card game in the Reception Saloon during the time of the battle, but he could never obtain corroboration of his alibi. The man he subpoenaed to verify his statement could not be found.

Bakersfield seethed with the excitement of the tragedy. A crowd gathered at Baer's Drug Store, and from the number of persons who later claimed to have talked to Will before he died it would almost seem that they talked him to death. When he was moved to the Southern Hotel, the crowd followed.

Another knot of curious citizens gathered at the Packard home, standing in the front yard to watch those who came and went and question them about the condition of the wounded man.

As word of Tibbet's death spread shortly after noon, a more sinister crowd assembled in the yard of the jail, and the ugly word "lynch" was heard frequently. Had not the jail presented such a formidable barrier, it is likely Hulse would not have survived the day. This same mob was all for marching in a body to burn the joss house and clean out other civic sores which fest-

ered in the tenderloin. Rumors of violence became so
common that Frank Rice, president of the board of
trade, was moved to make a public appeal to the people
of Bakersfield not to disgrace themselves by resorting
to mob action.

The city's two daily newspapers, the *Californian*
and the *Echo*, both issued extras bearing headlines in
the boldest woodblock type they could find in their
shops. When truth failed to provide them with illumi-
nating sidelights on the story, they printed rumors. The
Californian dug up a sentimental love interest angle,
carrying a story that the outlaw McKinney had a "lov-
ing wife" who had been with him in Randsburg and
Arizona and had written him affectionate letters. The
Californian also printed a tear-jerking yarn about Packard's little dog, Oscar, pining inconsolably at the death
of his master.

A reform hot-head, making a soapbox speech on a
street corner, with poorly timed stupidity suggested
that Bakersfield's vice was due to corrupt peace officers,
and that McKinney would have done the city a big
favor by killing them all. The reaction of his audience
was so violent that the speaker had to call on the very
peace officers he had assailed to protect him from the
crowd.

An oilfield worker, his sense of righteousness fired
with booze, took his shotgun and headed for the joss
house, telling friends he met along the way that he was
determined to exterminate single-handed the human
vermin he was sure still existed there. Fire Chief Gun-
lach, standing guard duty at the joss house to help pre-

vent such incidents, quenched the fire of the man's zeal by taking his shotgun away from him and sending him home to bed.

Bakersfield went to sleep that night surfeited with sensation. The battle in the joss house was to be the main topic of conversation for many days to come, and the *dramatis personae* were to contribute frequent new developments to keep the subject from becoming dull. The following morning word of the unexpected death of popular Jeff Packard spread about town, rekindling the indignation against Hulse.

The city council met in emergency session and appointed the hero of the hour, Burt Tibbet, the man who had beaten the notorious McKinney in a shotgun battle at deadly range, as Packard's successor as city marshal. Burt got together with Sheriff Kelly and the two began to map plans for the stamping out of vice and violence in response to public demand for reform. They also began rounding up everyone suspected of giving aid to McKinney during his flight from justice and while he was harbored in Bakersfield. The dragnet caught a numerous and motley group, and the jail was soon nearly filled, but under interrogation the charges of complicity failed to stand up, and all were eventually released.

The newspapers joined in the campaign for the cleanup so long overdue. "Our brothers have been sacrificed because the dens in Chinatown are haunted by humans of the lowest order," trumpeted the *Californian*. "The entire community is responsible."

It had words to say also on the quantity and variety of vice offered to the young men of Bakersfield. "The carnival of crime caused by McKinney could not have been charged to the mysterious dispensation of Providence, but rather to purely social and personal influences which tend to make young men go wild."

The *Californian* had a hand in furnishing the next sensational break in the case. In jail, Jenny Fox at first remained surly and refused to talk. A reporter from the *Californian* attempted to interview her, but got no story. However, he turned in a paragraph to the effect that the "French woman" was surprisingly attractive and appeared to be quite intelligent. If the reporter expected to win Jenny with flattery he was thoroughly successful. It is doubtful that Jenny had ever before been subjected to public compliment, and she reciprocated by calling in the sympathetic reporter the next day to give him a story which rated a well deserved banner headline:

"HULSE'S NECK IS IN THE NOOSE!"

It was the story she was to repeat at the inquest regarding her presence in the joss house when the shooting started, and that Hulse, McKinney, and a man unknown to her were also present. Those who expected Hulse to admit his guilt in the face of Jenny's damning statement were badly mistaken. Hulse hotly denied from his cell the truth of Jenny's confession and in injured innocence declared himself to be baffled by the treatment he was receiving from his old girl friend.

Three days after the shooting, the town turned out
en masse for the funerals of Packard and Tibbet. Services for Will were held at the Methodist Church, with
members of the Eagles lodge taking part, while the
Elks were eulogizing their departed brother at rites for
Jeff at the family residence on 18th Street. In the funeral sermons both men were praised for their courage
and devotion to duty, as well as for their virtues as good
fathers and husbands. In the crowded procession that
accompanied Packard's body to the cemetery, a horse
bolted and ran away, injuring a pedestrian.

After the coroner had satisfied himself with the examination of McKinney's body, it was turned over to
the outlaw's brothers, Ed and Jake, who had come to
Bakersfield to claim it. They instructed Payne & Hansberger to box it up and ship it north on the night train.
A Porterville mortician met the train at Pixley and trun-
dled the casket the twelve remaining miles to Porterville in a spring wagon. Tom Ferguson, who was later
to serve for many years as superintendent of the cemetery in which the outlaw's remains were deposited, was
on the train and was provoked that he had not been
asked to ride on the wagon from Pixley to Porterville,
for it would have saved him a long stop-over for a
change of trains at Goshen.

McKinney's body was taken to his mother's home on
Oak Street to be prepared by friends for burial. When
this last sad service was completed, the body lay on a
board cot in the humble parlor for the customary visi-
tations. Jim's many Porterville cronies, among them Kit
Tatman, came to Mrs. McKinney to volunteer their

196 •

services in "sitting up" with the body until the services were held. A steady stream of men and women came in to view the remains and console the mother. Chester Doyle was among those Mrs. McKinney personally escorted to the improvised bier, and she threw back the sheet that covered the body to the neck in order to show him the ugly wounds. Ugliest of all, in Doyle's opinion, was the wound on the chest the badman had received in the Canebrake Springs fight with McCracken and Rankin. Doyle did not know the coroner had made it appear worse by probing it.

One of Porterville's most prominent citizens was John A. Milligan, a minister of great versatility who could not only preach dynamically but was also a leader in the development of citrus packing and planting operations in the early days of the community's first industry. He was held in great esteem by people in all walks of life. His friends, in tribute to his sterling character, often referred to him as St. John. It was to him that Mrs. McKinney turned in her hour of sorrow to read the final rites for her scapegrace son.

The Rev. Mr. Milligan went to her home to offer words of comfort and to plan with Mrs. McKinney the final rites. "I was in the room for a brief time," he wrote years later, "and while there I noticed a large and powerfully built man come in. With just a word of greeting to me he passed to the side of the improvised bier, drew the sheet down from the face of the dead man, and stood there for some moments in silence looking at the dead face. Then I heard him say softly, 'Jim, you were a thoroughbred.'

● 197

"I did not know the man, only that he was one of Jim's pals. His words were a pal's eulogy, spoken in accordance with his conception of a thoroughbred. I did not find much in his lament to help me with the part I was expected to perform on the morrow.

"It was a difficult place to fill. It was not my mission to eulogize, berate or condemn McKinney. In the trail that led to his ending there was the blood from six killings attributed to him. It was my business to help a bereaved mother and brothers in what to them was a time of even greater sorrow than in the ordinary death and to render the service in such a manner that some hint from the words spoken might convey the idea that the way of the transgressor is hard.

"I was criticized by some for conducting a funeral for a man such as McKinney. I told one of my critics that the service was tragedy of both his life and his death; that the broken-hearted mother needed our help the more, the sadder the case might be."

As for Mrs. McKinney's feelings regarding her son and his evil deeds, there is the statement she is said to have made to a woman friend during her days of mourning.

"My Jim was a fine son, but when he drank he could, and would, kill."

Many months later Burt Tibbet came with his friend, Will Maston of Porterville, to call on Mrs. McKinney. Burt found the old lady wholly without resentment toward him, although she knew Burt to be the man who had fired the shots which ended her son's life.

Jim was laid to rest in the cemetery on the low hill just east of Porterville beside the body of his respected father. It was to be more than a quarter of a century before Mrs. McKinney would join them, and long before she did so the grave of her son, Ed, was to be close by.

•

•

XII

HAD HE known what his eventual fate was to be, it is certain Al Hulse would have chosen to die by the side of Jim McKinney on that fatal Sunday. From the day of his arrest, Hulse suffered the tortures of the damned and his life was a bitter turmoil. He was a confirmed narcotics user, and the enforced withdrawal of drugs which accompanied his incarceration had its usual physical and mental consequences for the big man. During his first weeks in jail, he was a raving, suicidal maniac for much of the time. He retched and vomited. He had terrible hallucinations. He screamed to his jailers that the Chinese were coming to cut his tongue out and chop him into small bits. His raving disturbed the other prisoners and could be heard a block away from

● 201

the jail, so he was moved from the airy second floor cell to an inside cell in the basement where he would cause less disturbance. There he cowered in the darkness and begged for weapons with which to defend himself against the myriad of demons his distorted brain conceived to persecute him. In desperation he yanked a bit of metal from his cot, sharpened it on the concrete floor, and attempted to cut his own throat, inflicting a jagged, painful wound. Thereafter he was allowed to have nothing in his cell with which he might harm himself, and his keepers maintained a close vigil on him. Despite their precautions, he almost succeeded in hanging himself with his bedclothing.

Yet somehow he managed to cling to sanity at critical times, and during moments of lucidity when he was questioned, he displayed a cunning which enabled him to match wits with the shrewdest of his inquisitors. When he was informed of Jenny's treachery, he requested an interview with the reporters who had been so sympathetic with Jenny and gave them such a logical account of his own activities during the fatal Sunday that a new note of respect for Hulse began to creep into the news columns.

"My word is as good as hers," he said to them in introducing his version of his activities.

He said that on the Thursday before April 19 he went to the Brewery Saloon for a drink, and after leaving there started up town. He admitted being an old friend of McKinney, saying that he had known him in Merced many years before.

"At L Street, either in front of Withington's or in front of the Palace," he said, "I stopped to talk to a woman. I heard a voice say 'Al, I want to talk to you.' Then I walked to the middle of the street and came face to face with McKinney.

"He said, 'Don't you know me, Al?' And I said, 'Of course I know you, Jim.' "

Then, related Hulse, McKinney told him he was worn out and asked to rest in Hulse's room for a couple of hours before leaving town.

"I told him he could, and we went down to the joss house together. He then said he wanted his guns. He had left them on the west side of the cemetery beneath the brush where the L runs out to the south."

Hulse described how he had gone to Fish's Livery Stable to rent a rig and admitted that he had threatened one of the attendants there with his gun after his request for a horse and buggy was rejected because of the lateness of the hour. He was able to make a deal with the attendant, however, and drove back to the joss house to pick up McKinney. Together they went to the cemetery, and because the night was quite dark, spent considerable time searching before they located the guns. They returned to the joss house. Hulse emphasized Jim's weariness by describing how the outlaw had walked thirty-five miles from Walker Basin over very rough country that day.

Hulse vehemently denied Jenny's statement that McKinney and Hulse planned to go to Arizona to lead lives of outlaws. McKinney had told him, Al said, that he wanted to get to Porterville, where he had been successful in hiding out for a considerable number of days after the Lynn killing.

"What was I to do?" Hulse asked the interviewers. "We were old friends and I am not an officer. I could see no harm in helping a friend in trouble. I would do the same thing again if it were to come up."

Hulse denied seeing McKinney at all on Friday but admitted sending several friends to the joss house at the outlaw's request. He said he had visited McKinney on Saturday and told of his efforts to obtain a suitable horse. He admitted purchasing ammunition for the weapons which had been recovered from the cemetery.

He went into detail regarding his movements on Sunday. He said he had gone out early, had taken breakfast in a restaurant, and had visited a barber shop. He repeated his contention that he had gone from the barber shop to the Reception Saloon and was watching a card game there when the gun battle was taking place at the joss house. He said that when he left the saloon, he encountered an acquaintance on the street who told him the sheriff wanted to see him for questioning as an accomplice in the shooting of Packard and Tibbet, and that was the first he knew of the affair.

Unlike almost everyone else in the area, he had not heard the commotion. He was hastening toward the scene to give himself up when he saw Kelly and Tower coming along L Street in their buggy.

"I am more sorry than I can say, not for myself, but for the men who were killed," Hulse declared.

The big man expressed his gratitude to the reporters for hearing his story, and he told them it was especially good to be in a lighter cell for the interview, as in his own dark, dungeon-like cell he had seen all sorts of ghastly things. He had calmed down to a considerable degree and was spending much time reading and preparing his defense. By April 30, the first day of the inquest, he was in good form.

Meanwhile, the reform movement inaugurated by the new marshal, Burt Tibbet, and Sheriff Kelly was beginning to show some results. They issued a joint statement that they would work hand in hand to rid the city of the vicious element which attracted such killers as McKinney. They raided eight or ten Chinese places which were suspected of dealing in gambling, prostitution, or opium. They served notice to the lords of the tenderloin to set their own houses in order or suffer the consequences. In this they were backed by resolutions from virtually every organization in town, including the machinists' union, urging that the rascals be thrown out. The *Californian* hailed their efforts as "the dawn of a new Bakersfield" which would become the epitome of civic virtue.

As a result, the night life in the tenderloin became less frantic almost at once. A good many of the worst offenders sought more convivial surroundings elsewhere. Violence, hitherto an almost nightly occurrence, ceased. It was said that for a time a man might walk safely through the darkest alley, his pockets bulging with gold, whereas before he would have been knocked in the head and robbed before he had gone a block. The girls stopped soliciting from their windows and on the streets, and gambling was relegated to the back rooms.

Men even quit wearing their six-shooters openly in their belts.

While Bakersfield was to be a hot spot for many years to come, so far as the sportier varieties of entertainment were to be concerned, it was never to slip quite back to the depths to which it had sunk when Packard and Tibbet were slain. It had a thriving red light district well into the 1930's, but it was a paragon of virtue in its method of operation compared to its counterpart of the earlier part of the century. The moving of military installations to the vicinity prior to the outbreak of World War II was to terminate, because of army insistence and the threat of putting the city "out of bounds" for military personnel, the open vice. The earthquake which hit Bakersfield in 1951 made necessary the removal of much of the physical evidence of the old days, helping to give the city a maturity which may well have begun in the joss house on L Street that sunny April morning of 1903.

On April 30 of that year, Coroner Mullins swore in at the old city hall a coroner's jury of respected Bakersfield citizens to hear the long and sensational testimony that was to be given. On the jury were E. M. Roberts, M. A. Duncan, E. P. Davis, Jess Minter, J. S. Drury, William Tyler, W. R. Coons, and G. C. Haberfelde. Most of the questioning was done by George Fluornoy, representing the district attorney.

Prominently on display at the inquest was a small arsenal of weapons which included a .25-.35 rifle and a 10-gauge shotgun said to belong to Hulse, a 12-gauge pump shotgun, a 10-gauge sawed-off shotgun, and a

.32-.40 Maynard rifle presumed to have been the property of McKinney; Will Tibbet's 12-gauge shotgun with a bullet gash on the stock, and Packard's damaged .30-.30 rifle.

Jenny Fox, prettier than usual after eleven days of good food, regular hours, and rest from her professional activities while an inmate of the county jail, was led into the jam-packed courtroom by Deputy Gus Tower. Her eyes avoided those of Hulse, who sat quietly beside a guard. Hulse was clean-shaven and wore a neat white sweater. He held his hat in his lap in such a manner that the manacles on his wrists were hidden.

Hulse set out with the first witness to strengthen his defense. After Sheriff Kelly had finished relating the events of the fatal day as he saw them, Hulse conducted a courteous cross-examination, mixing just enough humility into his innocent air to give the reporters a respect for his ability to influence a jury.

Hulse asked Kelly if he had seen anyone other than Chinese in the joss house, to which Kelly replied in the negative. Then he had the reluctant Kelly make a direct statement to the jury that Hulse's surrender had been voluntary and with no sign of resistance.

Then the crafty Hulse made a play for Jenny's sympathy. He asked Kelly if he had not told the sheriff while they were on their way to the jail that there was no use to blow up the joss house, as there was no one in it, and Kelly admitted Al had done so. This was Hulse's way of letting Jenny know that he was thinking of her safety if in truth he knew that she was locked in the closet at the joss house.

Burt Tibbet testified that as he bent over his brother's prostrate form, he had heard the sound of someone running across the floor of the cellar.

"Could it have been a Chinaman?" asked Hulse in his cross-examination.

"I don't know," was Burt's evasive answer.

Hulse continued to insist that Tibbet say whether or not he had seen Hulse in the joss house, and the new marshal was forced to admit that, despite his personal opinion regarding the presence of Hulse at the scene, he could not say that he had actually seen the big fellow. Burt merely could emphasize that Will had told him it was Hulse who shot him, and that Will had been shot with a rifle, while McKinney was armed with a shotgun.

Deputy Tower testified he had heard both Packard and Tibbet make statements that Hulse had shot them.

But it was Jenny's story which was the most damaging. She told the coroner's jury substantially the same story that she had related to the *Californian* reporter, that she had seen Hulse in the room and had seen him fire two shots before she ducked to safety behind the bed.

Hulse's approach to the cross-examination of his girl friend was so artfully pitched that it would have done credit to a highly skilled courtroom lawyer. Jenny was no fool, either, and her testimony lost none of its validity under Hulse's crafty probing.

Hulse asked her when she came to the joss house.

"You ought to know—you were there," she shot back quickly.

"What did you say your name was?" Hulse asked, sparring for an opening in her defensive attitude.

"You know," Jenny replied.

"That ain't what I'm asking you."

"Jenny Fox."

"Where do you live?"

"Any old place."

"That ain't what I'm asking you."

"I don't want to answer him," Jenny said, directing this statement to Fluornoy.

"Why are you so against me when you was once my friend?" Hulse appealed.

Jenny did not answer.

Hulse then accused her of having been prompted to give her story on the promise that by doing so she would be absolved of complicity in the killings. The woman vehemently denied it.

"No more questions," Hulse said with a sad shake of his head.

Other important testimony in the inquest linked Hulse directly to the shooting through statements attributed to the dying men.

"Al Hulse was the man who shot me," Ed Tibbet testified Will had told him at Baer's Drug Store.

"Get Hulse. He's the man who did the dirty work," Burt Tibbet quoted Jeff Packard as saying.

Hulse, in his cross-examination of Burt Tibbet, brought out that the deputies had blundered in picking up all the weapons and ruining other evidence at the joss house before a proper investigation could be made. This was to be a strong defense point in his later trials, when the inference was to be made that the officers scattered so much lead that it would be difficult to tell whether Packard and Tibbet were wounded by the outlaw McKinney or by the wild firing of their own companions.

Tower was certain he saw a white man run from the kitchen into a connecting room in the joss house in which there were several Orientals. Hulse demanded to know why one of these Chinese had not been produced as a witness to verify Tower's statement.

"They didn't say they saw me?" he taunted Tower with an air of mock incredulity. "They must have. Didn't they say so?"

Tower had to admit that none of the Chinese had told him they had seen a white man in the room.

Then Tower entered an objection with Coroner Mullins to the manner in which Hulse was attempting to ridicule him in the cross-examination.

Without waiting for Mullins to make a ruling, Hulse extended an exaggerated apology. "I ain't got no attorney and am not much of a cross-examiner, and if I ain't asking the questions exactly right, why it ain't my fault," he pleaded.

Etter, too, felt the sharp probe of Hulse's inquiry after Etter had testified briefly with an account of his experiences at the joss house. Hulse demanded to know if Etter had seen him in the joss house. Etter's reply was that the only time he had seen Hulse on the day of the battle was a half hour before Etter had joined the posse. He had seen Hulse getting a shave in a 19th Street barber shop.

Edward Willow, who had been with Packard as he was being taken away from the joss house, testified he had heard Jeff ask someone to "go down and get that son-of-a-bitch, Hulse." Richard Smith, another bystander when Tibbet was being treated at Baer's Drug Store, told of having heard Will make the statement that he had been shot by Hulse.

Dr. Shafer's testimony did Hulse's cause no harm. He said that during his conversations with Packard while he was treating his wounds he had heard Packard state definitely that he had seen McKinney aiming a gun at him, but Dr. Shafer said he could not remember that the marshal had once said that he had seen Hulse. The physician said Packard was amazed that he felt no pain when he was shot; his arms had suddenly refused to function and he was "blown right out of the house."

The jury was inclined to believe Jenny's assertion that Hulse was involved in the fight. In its verdict, it declared that death was "due to gunshot wounds inflicted by McKinney, Hulse, and another person unknown to this jury." To the verdict was appended a statement commending Burt Tibbet on his bravery and devotion to duty.

After the inquest, it was announced that all the surviving peace officers who had taken part in the joss house battle were renouncing their claims to the $2,000 reward in favor of the widows of the two dead men.

The arraignment and preliminary hearing for Hulse on charges of first degree murder in the court of Justice of the Peace W. S. Millard on May 9 added little to the evidence in the case. Jenny told her story again and this

time added that she had given Hulse $270 the day be-
fore the shooting, a touching indication of the loyalty
women of her profession felt toward the worthless characters who procured customers for them.

At the coroner's inquest Hulse had not taken the
stand in his own defense, and he chose not to do so at
the preliminary hearing. By May 9, he appeared much
improved in mental condition and again exhibited the
alert courtroom technique which prompted reporters
to repeat that he would have made a good attorney. He
was quick to catch the prosecution up in the confusion
over the guns collected by deputies at the scene of the
fight. He introduced a Chinese who claimed ownership
of a shotgun which Jenny identified as having been
used by McKinney in the fight. Another witness shook
Jenny's story by declaring two other weapons she said
were used had not been fired at all.

To add to the confusion, two men brought to the
stand to give prosecution testimony that they had seen
Hulse come out of the joss house cellar after the shooting, impeached their own testimony. One of the witnesses said Hulse was wearing a black hat. The other
witness was equally certain the hat worn by the man
was white. Someone was obviously confused.

Hulse also forced posse members to make the admission that they had left the front of the joss house un-
guarded when they all ran around to the back as the
shooting began. None had seen him come or go.

Despite these points, Judge Millard ordered Hulse
held to answer for trial without bail, and he went back
to his gloomy jail cell to endure once again his lonely

conflict with the evil creatures conjured up in his hallucinations while awaiting trial.

On June 16, nearly three months before the trial,
Jenny Fox burst back upon the front pages with a new
statement that rocked the prosecution and forced it to
rebuild its entire line of attack. She called in her sympathetic reporter from the *Californian* for an exclusive
interview in which she declared her previous story to
be largely a tissue of lies so far as Hulse's participation
was concerned.

She admitted that she was in the joss house, but, she
said, her only companion was the outlaw, Jim McKinney. Hulse and the third man were not there at all, according to her new version.

What prompted her to change her story is not clear.
Perhaps her decision was influenced by the realization
that she could only come out loser by violating one of
the few ethical traditions of her world, that of not being
an informer. She must have become convinced that it
would be most difficult to resume her former associations and ply her trade with the reputation of having
put her boy friend's head in the noose for no valid reason. Her very physical safety would have been in jeopardy. Perhaps she was also shrewd enough to realize
that the public clamor for vengeance on the slayers of
Packard and Tibbet was waning, and she was now safe
from prosecution as an accomplice. Her stated reason
for making the change was unconvincing.

"A person will say anything when she is in jail for the
first time," Jenny piously told the man from the *Califor-*

nian. "Hulse is the only man I care for and I will not go any farther to do him up."

Jenny made the most of the dramatic possibilities of her last appearance in the Bakersfield limelight by casting McKinney in the role of super gunfighter in the joss house battle.

She stated that she and McKinney were in the room alone when they heard Packard and Tibbet fumbling with the lock. McKinney, realizing a showdown was at hand, put all the guns in the center of the room, then knelt on one knee beside his weapons, facing the door.

When the door was flung open, Jim blazed away, changing from shotgun to rifle as the ammunition of the weapons became exhausted, one after another. Jenny said the outlaw made the same exclamations regarding "old Four-Eyes and old Overall" which she had attributed to him in her original story.

"I believe if he had not left the room he would have killed all the officers as fast as they came in the door," she said. "He left the room to protect me."

Her story lacked one essential factor to make it as plausible as her first version. She could not explain who had locked the door behind her after she had entered the closet.

She looked forward to telling her revised account in court, and exhibited a new-found vanity to the reporter who had befriended her. "I'm going to look like sweet sixteen in court," she told him. "I'll curl my hair and look pretty."

To his solicitous inquiry into the possibility of her reform, there was a firm answer.

"Will I give up the opium habit? No indeed! It is too much pleasure, and what have I to live for if not for pleasure?"

Jenny never had the opportunity to perform before the court, for she was not to be called as a witness by either side. What good to either would be the testimony of a person who, by her own admission, had lied under oath on two occasions? Jenny was soon released from jail to sink back into the morass of vice and dissipation from which her incarceration had temporarily liberated her, and it was soon to claim her body as well as her soul.

Jenny crossed back over the desert to resume what to her was "the life of pleasure." Three years later she was doing business in a tawdry saloon in Goldroads, one of the last of the frontier mining communities in the Territory of Arizona. Age and too much living had reduced her prestige in her profession, and the only man she could find to pimp for her was a worthless barfly as far gone in dissipation as herself.

One night she and her man engaged in a drunken argument in the saloon. Her consort pulled his gun and, in utter contempt of her worthless life, shot her. She fell face down on the dirty floor.

Before a horrified crowd of miners, her assailant began kicking at her prostrate body, and finally succeeded in turning it over. As her glazing eyes looked imploringly upward, he stepped astride her body and pumped the remaining bullets from his revolver full into her face.

It was as merciless a killing as Goldroads had ever seen and revolted the hardened miners to such a degree that they almost lynched the slayer before he could be hustled off to jail in Kingman. His conviction after trial and subsequent execution by hanging were mere formalities.

"We didn't have a gallows in Kingman, and in those days each county had to carry out its own hangings," Ace Harris recalled fifty years later.

"It was up to me, as undersheriff, to build the gallows. It was the custom to put three levers on the trip that sprung the trap. On the signal from the sheriff each man would pull a lever and none was supposed to know which of the three lever operators was the actual executioner. As undersheriff I had to operate one of the levers, but as the builder of the gallows I knew which was actually connected to the trap. I made certain I didn't get that lever."

The hanging drew a big crowd, as it was the last one Kingman was to enjoy. Future executions took place at the state capital.

Jenny had survived the vicissitudes of her calling much longer than most of her contemporaries, and her death, gruesome as it was, was far more merciful than the lingering agony that was to beset her old boy friend, Al Hulse, in his final months.

The men who had been in the gun fight did not believe Jenny's statement that McKinney, for all his acknowledged skill with firearms, was the only person in Hulse's room who fired a gun. Too many shots were fired in rapid succession from a variety of weapons to have been the work of one man.

216 •

Jenny's new story prompted the officers to abandon the search for the mysterious third man who was part of her original story. A good many men known to have visited McKinney at the joss house were picked up for questioning. Suspicion fell heaviest on a certain saloon operator from one of the mountain communities. He was arrested and released, then disappeared so he could not be subpoenaed for the trial of Hulse. In fact, several friends of McKinney and Hulse who were wanted as material witnesses found it prudent to be in the where-abouts-unknown category when the sheriff set out with subpoenas for the trial.

Without Jenny's testimony, the trial was anticlimactic. It took place in the court of Superior Judge J. W. Mahon in September of 1903. The court appointed two excellent attorneys, F. L. Alford and Rowan Irwin, to defend Hulse and they did a competent job, although it was scarcely better than the defendant could have done for himself. Their first step was to request a change of venue, arguing that it would not be possible to find in Kern County a jury whose members had not been subjected to the violent public sentiment that had followed the joss house killings. Much of the male population, they pointed out, belonged to either the Eagles or the Elks lodges and were thus fraternity brothers of either Packard or Will Tibbet. The defense further pointed out that Hulse must depend on the testimony of certain Chinese, and these were notably and justifiably reluctant to give evidence which might be offensive to a substantial portion of the white population

● 217

among whom the Celestials must dwell as members of a minority race.

Judge Mahon refused to grant the change of venue. The prosecution argued that while Hulse might have many persons against him, he also had a substantial number of sympathizers who believed his story and thought him to be the victim of a frameup.

J. W. P. Laird, who had successfully defended Mc-Kinney and kept him from accounting to society for the killing of Long Red Sears, was now on the other side of the table as district attorney in charge of the prosecution. He chose as his assistant Bert Packard, attorney brother of the dead marshal, who of course had strong personal feelings in the case.

First testimony submitted by the prosecution was by affidavit to the effect that there had been no mob violence around the jail, and that after the arrest of Hulse and Jenny Fox no more than a dozen men and boys had followed the prisoners to jail. The affidavits, given by Deputies Tower and Baker, certainly did not agree with the accounts carried in the two newspapers of the community at the time Hulse was jailed.

The first day of the trial was marked by another incident which almost brought about a mistrial. One of the jurors complained that he had been accused of taking a drink with Alford, the defense attorney, while court was adjourned for lunch, at the Anderson & Ross Saloon. The juror said he had protested to Alford when the attorney attempted to engage him in conversation.

"I've a good notion to swat you on the jaw," he declared he told Alford.

The attorney indignantly denied the implication that he had attempted to tamper with the jury. He said he merely asked the juror his name, as he had difficulty in remembering the identities of all the jurors.

The two important points in the trial were the attempts of the prosecution to place Hulse at the joss house and to establish as evidence the statements made by Packard and Tibbet before they died as the statements of men who knew themselves to be dying.

On the first point, Deputy Tower went farther than he had at the inquest or at the preliminary hearing. He testified he saw a white man, tall and wearing a white hat, go through the adjoining room as he entered the kitchen from the hall. His previous testimony had been that he had only heard a man go through the kitchen ahead of him, and evidence of his passing was the falling of a mush pot from the stove.

Three witnesses were brought to the stand to testify that they had seen a man at the corner of 21st and L Streets. None of the three could say positively that the man they had seen was Hulse, but all agreed there was a gun in the man's hand. Alford countered this testimony in the cross-examination by attempting to show that the man seen could have been Sheriff Lovin, who resembled Hulse in stature and wore a white hat.

Alford later called a defense witness, a woman, to testify that she had watched the front of the joss house all during the battle and had not seen Hulse leave. Alford also presented a witness to tell of having seen Hulse elsewhere in the tenderloin at the hour of the battle. Laird established that Alford's woman witness

• 219

was a prostitute by profession and asked the jury to ignore her testimony.

Hulse failed to establish his alibi that he was in the Reception Saloon watching a card game when McKinney was killed. He asked the court to bring to the stand a man who was supposed to have been at the Reception at the same time Hulse claimed to be there, but the sheriff was unable to locate the witness.

In the arguments over the establishment of the so-called deathbed statements of Packard and Tibbet, both prosecution and defense had some success. Deathbed statements are admissible as evidence although the person alleged to have made them is beyond cross-examination; the law assumes that a dying person, faced with accounting to the universal Judge, will speak only the truth.

The court had the testimony of both Burt Tibbet and Dr. Shafer that Packard had said Hulse was in the room, but Dr. Shafer was to prove an adverse witness for the prosecution. First of all, he established that anything Packard might have said could not be classified as the statement of a man who knew himself to be dying. The doctor pointed out that he did not believe Packard's wounds would be fatal and had assured the marshal that he would recover. When the doctor left Packard in the late afternoon on the day of the shooting, his patient was resting easily and was cheerful. Shafer was most amazed, he told the court, when he called back early the next morning and found the marshal in a deep coma and beyond aid.

The physician was also emphatic that he had never heard Packard, in all their conversation, say he had actually seen Hulse in the room, but had only inferred that he must have been there. On the other hand, Packard had been very definite in his statement that he had seen McKinney standing in the middle of the room. He apparently did not mention seeing Jenny Fox or anyone else.

In the case of Will Tibbet, the defense was not so successful. Burt, Ed, and the man named Morrow all testified that Will had said Hulse shot him, and there was little doubt that the grievously wounded man knew himself to be dying. He had asked Ed to remove his shoes, proof enough to any westerner that he knew himself to be at death's door.

The most effective testimony for the prosecution was that of Will's aged mother, Rebecca Tibbet, a frail pioneer whose quiet dignity and straightforward account of her last conversation with her dying son at Baer's Drug Store had a powerful effect on those in the courtroom.

Hulse, sitting at the table for the defense, visibly blanched as he became aware of the influence this little lady who resembled everybody's ideal mother was having on the jury. He shuddered at her grim quotation of her son's statement, "Hulse shot me."

Laird led her carefully into establishing that Will knew himself to be dying.

"How is it with your soul, my son?" Mrs. Tibbet said she had asked Will.

"I have made my peace with God," was Will's reply to her.

Laird asked her if Will had made a direct statement that he knew his condition would terminate in death. Mrs. Tibbet quoted as Will's exact words: "I am dying. I am suffering terribly. I can't stand it."

But even such emotionally charged testimony was not sufficient to convict Hulse. The prosecution could offer no one on their side who had heard either Will or Jeff say he saw Hulse standing in the room pointing and firing a gun. They placed Hulse in the room only by inference, for it seemed logical to assume that Mc-Kinney alone could not have produced the withering blast of shotgun and rifle fire that burst full upon them when the door swung open. Yet the prosecution had not proved that it was Al Hulse who had been there to help McKinney.

Another weakness of the prosecution was its failure to produce a single witness who would say unequivocably and irrefutably that he had seen Hulse inside the joss house during or after the battle or had seen him leave the place by way of the front door.

The jury, after many hours of deliberation, came out hopelessly deadlocked. The vote was seven to five for acquittal.

XIII

Hulse, the man whom Bakersfield would have gladly lynched on the afternoon of April 19 if its citizens could have gotten their hands on him, had won a victory, but it was to be an empty one—perhaps even worse than conviction and a death sentence would have been for Hulse's tortured soul.

A few weeks later, Al stood trial again. Laird and Bert Packard drafted a third attorney, Thomas Scott, to help them with the prosecution. The testimony was much the same as it had been in the first trial, but the prosecution concentrated its emphasis on demonstrating that even if Hulse was not in the actual gun battle, he was certainly an accessory to the deaths of Packard and Tibbet for having given aid and comfort to McKinney.

Hulse made one grave error when he tried to deny that he knew McKinney was wanted for murder in Porterville and Arizona. It was almost an insult to the jury for Hulse to think its members would be sufficiently naive to believe he could have failed to hear about a sensational story of the magnitude of the one relating to Jim McKinney's escapades. While he would not admit knowing McKinney was a wanted man, he did confess to sheltering him in his room, buying medicine for his wound, and procuring ammunition for his guns as well as a horse for his escape.

The jury brought in a conviction of second degree murder, and Judge Mahon sentenced Hulse to life in Folsom prison.

Although Hulse was to survive another three years, he was never to serve any of his time in prison. Alford appealed the case and won a stay of execution of sentence. The appellate court took its time mulling over the evidence, and while the months dragged on, Hulse languished in the Kern County jail, hoping for a new trial. Alford died, and Irwin took over the case. Still there was no decision from the appellate court.

Hulse, in the monotony of waiting, was revisited by fits of mental depression which he had exhibited when he was first jailed, but which had subsided during the stress of his two trials. Once again he battled imaginary enemies in the darkness of his cell, and he screamed out in the night until the jailer came to banish his tortures by turning on the light. He had little peace in the daytime, for then he could hear mysterious voices threatening his life.

"He has ingeniously prepared a contrivance to hear these voices better," the *Californian* reported in a routime check on his welfare.

The months stretched out into years, and because of Hulse's mental condition, there was no need for the court to hurry its decision. He was no longer able to comprehend the legal procedures. Friends who visited him found him "quite gone."

Whatever the state of his reasoning processes, his craftiness remained. Because of his frequent threats and attempts at suicide, his jailers became accustomed to making sure he had nothing about him which could be used as a fatal instrument. He was allowed to shave once a week, but when he did so, someone stood by him to make sure he used the razor only to cut his beard.

In October of 1906, his threats of self-destruction became more frequent as the voices he heard in his cell became more terrifying.

On the afternoon of October 15 he told his fellow prisoners: "Thank you for all you have done for me. It is all off with me today."

It was the day for shaving. When Hulse's turn came to use the razor, he seemed unusually rational and cheerful. Something of his old disarming personality seemed to have returned. He joked with his fellow prisoners and the jailer. When his time came to use the razor, he took the instrument and, after lathering his face, began to use it. He made some remark about excusing himself and walked away to the lavatory of the jail and there quickly slashed his throat from ear to ear. He staggered and fell with his head in the trough of the

• 225

urinal at one end of the room. His fellow prisoners heard his gasps, and when the jailers rushed in to pick him up, his head nearly fell off. He had ended his own misspent life at the age of 41.

Thus ended the last life that Jim McKinney, last of the western badmen, was to be responsible for terminating—for had Al Hulse not fallen into the company of McKinney, his death might have been less horrible.

*   *   *

*   *   *

*   *   *

XIV

It is not possible to dwell upon the evil career of such a man as James McKinney without speculating on the terrible waste of human resource which is always the greatest tragedy of the diversion of a zest for living into debauchery. McKinney's friends who are still living as this is written are most apt to say when his name is mentioned, "He was the finest man I ever met," and then, with a shake of the head, add "but he had such a terrible temper when he was drinking."

Of course, their evaluation is made without the consideration of the true nature of the man which led him to murder two of his best friends, Red Sears and Billy Lynn; to ambush two total strangers and kill them in cold blood, and finally to become a cop-killer in the blasting of Will Tibbet and Jeff Packard.

The big man who stood over McKinney's body and said in the presence of John Milligan, "Jim, you were a thoroughbred," could not have been thinking of his maniacal outbursts. Nor could he have been thinking of the parasitic manner in which the outlaw made his living by gambling, hiring out as a shotgun man, and by sharing the earnings of the unfortunate prostitutes for whom he procured. A friend viewing him in death might have remembered his good points, including his generosity with those who were down and out, his quiet, courteous manner when he was sober and not aroused, his notable skill with horses, and his regard for his mother.

Had McKinney been in control of his passions, he might well have gone down in the history of the west not as its last badman, but as a successful man who helped to build it in the field of some worthy endeavor. So far as can be determined, neither he nor his brothers established families to carry on their name.

The grass grows green in the Porterville cemetery where he lies in the company of respected people, and not with his own kind on some notorious Boot Hill such as was the fate of many of his predecessors among western badmen. There is no marker on his grave, but its location can be determined by the stone that honors his parents.

The house where Sarah lived in Porterville is gone, as is the house where Jim's mother lived and received his torn body. Scotty's Chop House burned to the ground in 1903 and was rebuilt as a pool hall; today old men sit and play cards for small stakes where Jim Mc-

Kinney stopped the electric fan with one shot from his six-gun. Police drop in for friendly chats with those who tend the pool hall without fear of encountering a drunken maniac with a gun in his belt.

In Bakersfield, the joss house is gone. In its place the Ying Ming Association, respectable successor to the old tong, has built a neat, modern structure with delicate Oriental architectural decoration which Occidentals find charming to look at as well as useful to members of the lodge. Its members come and go in their late model automobiles, pursuing legitimate businesses and contributing to the life of their community. The only smoking done there today is by means of peaceful tobacco pipes clamped in the teeth of placid members who no longer need escape life's reality in poppy dreams. The manager, a native of Bakersfield now more than sixty years old, will tell the stranger of the vast change for the better which has occurred in the neighborhood since he, as a little boy, fished for perch in the irrigation ditch that once ran down the side of L Street.

The earthquake of 1951 wiped out most of the old buildings which had served the tenderloin. New buildings have replaced them or the sites have been converted into parking lots for the too-numerous automobiles of the citizens of the booming city which has grown in recent years at a pace it never matched when it operated as the most "wide open" town in the nation. Where Tom Owens operated Bakersfield's biggest gambling hall, his son and grandson have the largest toy store in the San Joaquin Valley and Tom's son, Charlie, likes his city better the way it is today than the way it was when he was a boy.

To those old enough and sufficiently worldly wise, there is one building remaining in the tenderloin which may be identified from its architecture as having been built to serve a gay business whose chief merchandise was a supply of loose-moraled floozies. The individual cribs of this building are shown by the window where the prostitute sat to give the come-on to the customers and the door by which the patron entered. It was in the alley near this building that Tom Sears so recklessly invited McKinney to shoot him on Friday the 13th, 1901.

The Old West passed in Bakersfield. The beginning of the end was that Sunday morning in April when Burt Tibbet exterminated the last of the old-style badmen with two well-aimed blasts of his shotgun.

CPSIA information can be obtained
at www.ICGtesting.com
Printed in the USA
BVHW042002280621
610669BV00014B/476